THE UNCOMMON MARRIAGE ADVENTURE

THE UNCOMMON MARRIAGE *adventure*

a daily journey to draw you closer to God and each other

TONY & LAUREN DUNGY

WITH NATHAN WHITAKER

TYNDALE MOMENTUM

An Imprint of
Tyndale House Publishers, Inc.

Visit Tyndale online at www.tyndale.com.

Visit Tyndale Momentum online at www.tyndalemomentum.com.

TYNDALE, *Tyndale Momentum*, and the Tyndale Momentum logo are registered trademarks for Tyndale House Publishers, Inc. UnCommon is a trademark of Tyndale House Publishers, Inc. Tyndale Momentum is an imprint of Tyndale House Publishers, Inc.

The Uncommon Marriage Adventure: A Daily Journey to Draw You Closer to God and Each Other

Designed by Dean H. Renninger

Published in association with the literary agency of Legacy, LLC, Winter Park, Florida 32789.

ISBN 978-1-4143-8372-9

Printed in the United States of America

20	19	18	17	16	15	14
7	6	5	4	3	2	1

INTRODUCTION

Before we married, we made a simple choice that has had a profound impact on our lives.

Rather than looking to the world for wisdom on building a strong marriage, we chose to listen to God. That one decision has enabled us to endure—and even thrive—through the best and worst of times. And considering how much society's views on marriage have changed in the thirty-plus years we've been married, we're thankful for biblical principles that are both unchanging and unassailable.

That's why, when we agreed to tell our story in our earlier book *Uncommon Marriage*, we chose to think about it from a couple of different angles. Yes, we spent hours reminiscing and telling stories about our years together. But once the chronological events had been laid out, we decided to look at our story in another way—by considering the core biblical principles behind it.

From those discussions, we developed "The Core Principles of an Uncommon Marriage," which you'll find on page ix. When we examined those principles further, we realized that a number of practices—specific actions we've taken to live out those principles—emerged as well.

As we said in *Uncommon Marriage*, we don't claim that our

list is exhaustive. However, we believe it may be a helpful tool for any couple who wants to explore the biblical principles related to marriage.

Those core principles and practices also provide the framework for this devotional, which is designed to be used over sixteen weeks and can be started any time of the year. We spend two weeks considering each of the eight core principles. Days 1 through 6 take a closer look at one of the practices related to that principle. Each of those devotionals ends with what we call an Adventure Application—a conversation starter or a simple activity you can do to explore that practice further.

Day 7 allows you to reflect and use the prayer prompts to ask for God's help in a particular area. You'll also be encouraged to choose one of the Adventure Applications to concentrate on further that week. You might find you'd like to work on several things, but we urge you to choose just one. If you'd like, jot a note to the side to remind you of another practice you'd like to try. Then feel free to come back to it in the fifth month, or to go through the book again and try other action items.

We wrote this book to encourage you not to give up hope on your marriage, no matter what shape it's in today. Perhaps you're looking just to tweak a good relationship. We're thrilled and hope you find an idea or two in these pages to help.

Or you may have picked up this book because you're discouraged. You've lost the spark in your marriage. You're bored. Your spouse is busy. (Or vice versa.) If that describes you, remember that *you are not alone*. Use this book as a tool to help you work together to make your marriage stronger. As you do, remember this promise in Scripture: "Let's not get tired of doing what is good. At just the right time we will reap a harvest of blessing if we don't give up" (Galatians 6:9).

Maybe you are engaged or thinking about it, but you wonder if marriage is even a big deal. *I love her; who cares if it's official?*

We've found the concept of commitment to be incredibly powerful. It helps us remember: *We're in this together. For better or worse. Now let's press on.* As you use this devotional, we think you'll better understand why the vows we make in marriage fortify our resolve to persevere when the going gets tough.

No matter where you are in your relationship, you (like us) need God's grace and direction every day. After all, the gospel of Jesus Christ says we are to be transformed . . . but it doesn't say that change will be immediate. And it doesn't promise that we won't make the same mistakes as a husband—or a wife—over and over.

But Scripture does promise a new life when we decide to follow Christ. A life of abundance . . . and grace. As some of you may recognize, *grace* in this context means "the unmerited—unearned—favor of God." All we need to do is ask for it.

Remember this—life is an adventure. If it were easy, we'd have it figured out, and we wouldn't be sharing our challenges here in these pages. And like any undertaking, the joy and fulfillment that come from working together will make the hard work worthwhile.

So press on.

Pray together.

Don't give up.

Our prayer is that as you read *The Uncommon Marriage Adventure*, you will rejoice over your partnership even as you wrestle with ways you might improve it—just as we did as we wrote this devotional.

May the Lord bless and keep you *and* your marriage.

Tony and Lauren Dungy
June 2014

THE CORE PRINCIPLES
OF AN UNCOMMON MARRIAGE

1. Look to the Bible as your guidebook
   and to Christ as your living example.

2. Stay in sync spiritually.

3. Manage expectations and appreciate
   your differences.

4. Work as a team.

5. Practice committed love.

6. Communicate well and often.

7. Don't run away from conflict.

8. Support each other in serving others.

day 1
AT THE CENTER

CORE PRACTICE #1:
Make Christ the center of your marriage.

....

Is there any encouragement from belonging to Christ? Any comfort from his love? Any fellowship together in the Spirit? Are your hearts tender and compassionate? Then make me truly happy by agreeing wholeheartedly with each other, loving one another, and working together with one mind and purpose. —PHILIPPIANS 2:1-2

Lauren

When Tony served as a head coach in the NFL, the coaches' wives often visited classrooms in inner-city schools to read to and talk with students. This practice continues to be one of my priorities, and now that Tony is retired, he has joined me. We have visited two third-grade classrooms in the heart of Tampa almost every Tuesday since 2009.

After we finish reading one of our books to the students, we take their questions. At first, some of the inquiries surprised us. "Are you two married? To each other?" We've learned to expect surprised looks or exclamations like, "Wow, you're kidding me!" when we tell them that, yes, we've been married for more than thirty years.

My favorite question came from a boy who eagerly raised his hand and asked, "Are you guys Christians?" I felt such joy that a third grader recognized our love for God and desire to follow His plan.

Tony and I have fulfilled many roles during our marriage: spouse, parent, coach, teacher, speaker, and broadcaster, to name just a few. Yet nothing is more important than being Christ followers. Christ is also the center of our marriage—the source of love, grace, forgiveness, and perseverance we need to make it through each day.

During most of my single life I hadn't been focused on getting married. But when my thoughts finally drifted to marriage and *whom* I might marry, I knew I wanted to marry a Christian—an authentic, deeply committed, passionate, and growing follower of Christ.

When I met Tony, I learned he did too.

We both felt blessed to have parents who were happily married as well—we knew that was unusual. Within our circle of family and friends, Tony and I had numerous other examples of couples with great marriages because they were following biblical principles. Those principles guided not only their decision making, but also helped them as they raised their children, developed friendships and other associations, handled their finances, and became active in churches. We had also seen how some couples with different faith walks or none at all sometimes struggled to navigate the challenges of marriage. They lacked a common source of wisdom and grace.

Striving to keep Christ at the center of our relationship has been and continues to be the key to building our marriage. He is the source of true and lasting encouragement, comfort, and love, which makes it possible for us to set aside our selfish interests and live in ever-increasing harmony. Tony and I like to remind couples that the process of two becoming one may begin on their wedding day, but that is just the beginning of a lifetime journey of commitment. We never stop growing with and learning about each other.

Maybe it's because I once taught math as a sixth-grade teacher, but one of my favorite analogies of a Christ-centered marriage is an equilateral triangle. As you may recall from geometry class, all three sides of an equilateral triangle are the same length. (See? Your teacher *told* you you'd be using this later!) I picture Christ at the top of the triangle. The bride and groom, respectively, form the other two corners. The only way for a married couple to grow closer to each other is for each to grow closer to Christ—shortening the sides of the triangle. And making Christ the focus of one's relationship is all part of God's inviolate plan for marriage.

While our journey hasn't been perfect every moment, Tony and I have always known that whenever we start to get off track, whenever we feel strain or tension, we can turn toward our center and draw closer to Christ—and thereby to each other.

Adventure Application: Take a moment to each draw a triangle. Be sure the sides reflect the distance you currently feel between each other and Christ. (The longer the sides, the further apart you feel.) Now compare your triangles. Discuss why you drew them the way you did, and how focusing on Christ could shorten the sides and bring you closer together.

day 2
LOVING YOUR IN-LAWS

CORE PRACTICE #2:
Treat your parents and others in authority with respect.

....

Honor your father and mother. Then you will live a long, full life in the land the LORD your God is giving you. —EXODUS 20:12

Lauren

I come from a talkative, expressive family, so early in our marriage, I wondered what the quiet, reserved Dungys really thought about me. Tony, on the other hand, quickly learned to accept brutally honest advice from my father and brothers—whether or not he'd asked for it. More than once, Tony and I had to sit down to discuss our families' differences as we figured out how to love and honor our in-laws.

Sometimes we even had to laugh—such as the afternoon I told Tony how I'd nearly fainted from the heat after taking his dad outside to show him our new vegetable garden. I'd asked Wilbur Dungy a simple question about how far apart to plant green beans, only to have him launch into a two-hour lecture on soil content and photosynthesis. That's the day I learned my father-in-law would open up—as long as you were talking about something he was passionate about!

Given our experiences, whenever I am at a wedding I wonder if the bride and groom fully understand that they are not only gaining a spouse, they are inheriting an extended family. Because that is what happens when a bridal couple enters into the sacred covenant of marriage. Despite adding "in-law" to each name, the truth is that every new bride and groom in essence has a new "mother" and a new "father."

All too often, brand-new married couples are unsure how to deal with their in-laws. I like how Gary Chapman, author of *The 5 Love Languages*, frames their predicament. Couples, he says, must balance two principles: leaving their parents while still honoring them. The Bible makes it clear that "a man leaves his father and mother and is joined to his wife, and the two are united into one" (Genesis 2:24). But while a couple's allegiance shifts from their parents to each other, they are to continue to honor their parents, to value their wisdom, and to seek their best. If the admonishment to "honor your father and mother" in Exodus 20:12 is not enough for a husband to treat his wife's parents as his own—and vice versa for his bride—then the respect due to each other should be enough to carry the day.[1]

The way we treat our parents affects more than our own relationship with them. A speaker at our church recently pointed out that one of the biggest problems in America is that we have not been trained well in how to honor our fathers and mothers as the Bible commands. As a result, we don't have proper attitudes toward those in authority. Yet even when we don't like the behavior modeled by a leader, we have to respect the position of authority he or she holds. That's a lesson Tony and I want our kids to learn. We want to ensure they honor us and develop proper respect for other authority figures, whether or not they like everything those in charge do.

Loving your in-laws is much easier when you start with honor and respect.

Adventure Application: Is there an issue you need to discuss with your spouse about either set of your parents? Talk about how Exodus 20:12 and Genesis 2:24 speak to that issue.

day 3
FOR GOD SO LOVED . . .

CORE PRACTICE #3:
Husbands: Work hard to hear your wife's heart and meet her needs.

For God loved the world so much that he gave his one and only Son, so that everyone who believes in him will not perish but have eternal life. God sent his Son into the world not to judge the world, but to save the world through him. —JOHN 3:16-17

TONY

Bill McCartney was a longtime college football coach whom I first got to know while playing high school football in Michigan, where I grew up. Bill would later coach at the University of Colorado, where he led the Buffaloes to their only national title. In 1990, he felt called to something different and started Promise Keepers, a ministry movement that reaches out to men.

Shortly after Bill founded Promise Keepers, the organization held a men's conference at Houlihan's Stadium in Tampa. Bill was one of the speakers. I had just been hired by the Tampa Bay Buccaneers as their head football coach, and I attended the conference along with several members of my staff. Bill's message impacted me then and continues to carry weight and meaning with me today.

Bill told us that he had started Promise Keepers because of a mistake he had made in his marriage. He admitted that he'd been so shortsighted and self-centered in his drive to become a successful college football coach that he'd often disregarded his wife's needs. Lindy had never balked or failed to support him as he pursued his passion for a career in the world of sports.

However, in the process, she never had the chance to pursue her individual dreams. Even worse, Bill confessed that he'd never given Lindy's desires much thought, figuring that she'd understood when they married that she needed to stand by his career.

When Bill really looked into his wife's eyes, he realized that the life had gone out of them. He resolved to begin serving her. After telling his story, he challenged us to read John 3:16— a Scripture reference familiar to many sports fans—in a new way. He said that when he replaced the words *the world* in that verse with Lindy's name, his attitude toward her had completely changed.

As we left the stadium that day, my fellow coaches and I talked about how Bill's message had resonated with every one of us—because we had done the very same thing with our careers and to our wives. We realized that as we had reached for our dreams, our marriages became a "one-way street," and we expected our wives to support the destination we had chosen. That night, we left the conference vowing to change that paradigm.

In today's Scripture passage, Jesus told Nicodemus, a curious religious leader, that God so loved the world that He gave His one and only Son as a sacrifice. That verse took on new meaning for me in the stadium that day. As I followed Bill's example, I read the passage like this: "For God loved *Lauren* so much that he gave his one and only Son, so that if *Lauren* believes in him, [she] will not perish but have eternal life." Reading it that way allowed me to see Lauren, the woman whom the King of kings had arranged for me to marry, in a new light. More than ever, I wanted my actions and attitude to give her a lift and ongoing encouragement.

When we put the names of our loved ones, friends, and others who cross our paths into this passage, they take on sacred significance. In our minds and hearts, we begin to view them as God has always seen them—as prime objects of His love and caring affection. Then we are better able to help them become all they were created to be, to follow their dreams and to use their gifts for their good and the good of others.

Adventure Application: Read John 3:16 aloud, inserting your wife's name where appropriate. How does that help you better appreciate God's love for her? How does it impact your attitude toward her?

day 4
CAUGHT IN THE MIDDLE

CORE PRACTICE #4:
Husbands: Be prepared to love sacrificially.

....

For husbands, this means love your wives, just as Christ loved the church. He gave up his life for her to make her holy and clean, washed by the cleansing of God's word. —EPHESIANS 5:25-26

TONY

Long airplane rides. Turbulent, stormy weather. Middle seats in a row of three.

Those are just a few of the hassles that can come with regular airline travel. Because of my coaching jobs, I have done a lot of flying over the years. Lately those trips have included going cross country from our home in Tampa to Oregon to watch our son play football. The window seat is my preference when I travel by myself. To make the trip as pleasant as possible, I see to it that I arrive and check in early, board the plane when called, and then settle into my seat and relax.

But that is only when I fly alone. When I fly with Lauren, all my personal plans and preferences, well, they end up out the window. Because we prefer to sit together, we know that whenever our plane's seat configuration has rows of three, one of us is going to have to sit in the middle seat. Lauren doesn't fly as much as I do, but I know how much she loves sitting by the window!

From this vantage point, she can see what is happening on the tarmac below, watch other flights take off and land, make sure—when possible—that our luggage has been loaded, and observe any changes in the weather. Once airborne, she tries to identify locations in the town we just took off from, view the beautiful countryside as the jet soars by, and take in all the gorgeous cloud formations. (And if she wants to sleep, she can put her pillow against the window and not worry about an awkward interaction with a stranger.)

You know what I mean when I say that the middle seat doesn't offer a lot of privacy. Sitting there can make you feel cramped and uncomfortable. Especially when the person in front of you decides to recline. Taking the middle seat is definitely a sacrifice. And between Lauren and me, it is a sacrifice of love. I think Jesus would be pleased, considering His admonition in the Sermon on the Mount that "if anyone would sue you and take your tunic, let him have your cloak as well. And if anyone forces you to go one mile, go with him two miles" (Matthew 5:40-41, esv).

I realize that having to give up the window seat for Lauren doesn't rise anywhere near the examples of sacrifice that Jesus gives. But in all cases, the attitude of our heart determines whether or not we willingly set aside our wants for another. The lesson of the middle seat is simply another way to remember my responsibility to serve others, just as Christ came to serve—not to be served.

Loving sacrificially requires a willingness to surrender every need, every desire, every right, and every position and claim of our own for the good of our spouse or others without begrudging them. God calls upon me to demonstrate sacrificial love to my wife. That simply means that I recognize and put her first in everything—even when it means giving up my window seat.

Adventure Application: How do you define *sacrifice*? In what ways do you sacrifice and "take the middle seat" so your spouse can feel loved?

day 5
THE ONE THING YOU CAN CONTROL

CORE PRACTICE #5:
Wives: Show love and respect to your husband.

....

In the same way, you wives must accept the authority of your husbands.
Then, even if some refuse to obey the Good News, your godly lives will
speak to them without any words. They will be won over by observing
your pure and reverent lives. —1 PETER 3:1-2

Lauren

I learned a long time ago that the circumstances of my day often dictate my attitude. They can determine whether my day is going to be sunny or cloudy—no matter what the weather actually is.

My personal situation may affect how I make decisions and color my perception of comments I hear others make. They frequently determine what comes out of my mouth in response to what others say or what is happening around me.

My circumstances are that powerful. The question is: Do they have to be?

In his book *Man's Search for Meaning*, Viktor Frankl recounts the unspeakable horrors of his longtime imprisonment in Nazi concentration camps like Auschwitz and Dachau. As a prisoner, he was stripped of everything. His father, mother, brother, and wife all died in similar prison camps. Though he survived, Frankl suffered from hunger, cold, and brutality. He had lost every possession and knew he could be killed at any hour, but he still found value and hope in his day. Life, he discovered, was worth preserving.

Even in our most desperate circumstances, he noted, we are never stripped of the "last of human freedoms: to choose one's attitude in any given set of circumstances."[2] In other words, though we can't always choose our situation, we can always choose our attitude—which makes it possible for us to rise above those circumstances.

That's a healthy, relationship-enhancing reminder for me as I strive to show love and respect to Tony—even on those days when what's going on around me leaves me feeling tired, overlooked, or annoyed. When our two oldest children were small, Tony took a job coaching the defensive backs for the Kansas City Chiefs. During the season, he often didn't return home until 2:00 a.m. That meant I had to run the home on my own for much of the year. If the car broke down, I took it to the garage. If one of the kids was struggling in a class, I contacted the teacher. If the lawn needed mowing, I took care of it.

As difficult as that was, it was almost harder when the season ended. As you can imagine, Tony was anxious to reconnect with the kids—which sometimes meant disrupting their homework and bedtime schedule. Even though I knew his heart was in the right place, I was frustrated. After I'd spent months establishing household rules, was it right for Tony to disturb them just because he wanted to take the kids out for ice cream?

But other than blowing off some steam, what would I have gained by lashing out at Tony? What would I have taught the kids about working out differences and honoring others within our home? I realized that I always had the choice, no matter what was going on or how I felt about Tony's actions, to control my response. I had the choice as to how I would react. I wanted to win over my family, to model in some small way

God's extravagant love and forgiveness. That often meant I had to check my words and my attitudes.

If we show our spouses the respect they deserve in spite of our circumstances, we can make a difficult moment better. The apostle Peter says that when wives demonstrate love for their husbands by respecting their position, they may win their husbands over without the use of words. Who knows? That might even encourage husbands to respond to us with increased love and affection.

Adventure Application: Offer a sincere compliment about your spouse this week in front of your children, your parents or siblings, or your friends at church, at work, or in the neighborhood. If possible, do it when he is there too!

day 6
VOLUNTARY SUBMISSION

CORE PRACTICE #6:
Wives: Strike the right balance between acceptance and expressing your disappointment when following your husband's lead in an area where you disagree.

For wives, this means submit to your husbands as to the Lord.
—EPHESIANS 5:22

Lauren

When Tony and I first talked about moving to Minnesota in 1992, we viewed the situation much differently. It was a good opportunity for him professionally since he would become the Vikings' defensive coordinator; however, I didn't see how this move would benefit our family. During our three years in Kansas City, we had connected with so many people, and we had found a phenomenal church. The community was an ideal fit for all of us.

In the end, Tony made the decision to accept the position, even though he knew going to Minnesota was not my choice. I felt that we hadn't discussed the decision sufficiently, nor had we prayed about it enough individually and together. I shared my concerns with Tony.

But ultimately I was ready to follow God's direction in submitting to what Tony felt was the right decision, honoring him and also demonstrating my love for him in that process. Don't get me wrong; it wasn't easy then, and I still consider it to be one of the most difficult times in our marriage.

So I understand why this passage has negative connotations.

Whenever someone speaks of or debates this verse, feelings can get intense on both sides.

I believe that's partly because much of the submission we have witnessed in human history has been forced. People who have been captured by military action or enslaved by others have been required to submit to stay alive. The dominating party has received all the benefits in these one-way relationships to the detriment of those who have had to obey. That's what most of us think of when we hear the term *submission*, and we understandably balk at those applications.

However, that is not what the apostle Paul was describing when he wrote this letter to the believers at the church at Ephesus. He was advocating *voluntary* submission, which occurs when people decide on their own to come under the protection and guidance of another for *their* benefit. This type of submission forms the whole basis for Christian marriage. The husband voluntarily puts himself under Christ's direction and guidance, submitting his will to that of Jesus. And the wife likewise puts herself under the direction of Jesus and her husband. When this happens, both parties receive the benefits of following Christ, together.

Remember that Christ lived out submission by following His Father's will for His life, mission, and purpose. Christ came, ministered to those all around Him, died on the cross for you and for me, and rose from the tomb to assure eternal salvation for all who believe in Him. His sacrifice culminated in the new covenant between God and His people.

When we follow that example in our marriages, not only will we glorify God, but our obedience will allow us to ultimately see the blessings God has for us. As I look back at our years in Minnesota, I see many blessings. For example, I made some wonderful friendships that continue to this day. Tony further established his abilities and experience as an exceptional coach, and our children got to connect and bond with a few of their cousins who lived nearby.

And the next time Tony and I had to decide whether to move, we approached it differently. We had both learned what it meant to honor and submit to each other, so we spent more time deliberating and praying together about our decision. Of course, the fact that we were moving to sunny Florida made it much easier!

Adventure Application: Submission can be a loaded term in our culture. Take a few minutes today to discuss what this word means to you. Do you each feel that the other hears your heart and respects your feelings? If not, godly submission will be tough to practice. How might you begin to practice submission and meeting your spouse where he or she is?

day 7

PRINCIPLE 1

LOOK TO THE BIBLE AS YOUR GUIDEBOOK AND TO CHRIST AS YOUR LIVING EXAMPLE.

UNCOMMON WISDOM

Submit to one another out of reverence for Christ. —EPHESIANS 5:21

UNCOMMON PRACTICE

Take a few moments to select one of this week's practices to explore further. Or you may each want to choose one principle directed specifically to you as the husband or you as the wife.

The related Adventure Application appears just below each practice. If you'd prefer to come up with a different way of living out that practice this week, feel free to discuss what that might look like.

- *Make Christ the center of your marriage.*
  Take a moment to each draw a triangle. Be sure the sides reflect the distance you currently feel between each other and Christ. (The longer the sides, the further apart you feel.) Now compare your triangles. Discuss why you drew them the way you did, and how focusing on Christ could shorten the sides and bring you closer together.

- *Treat your parents and others in authority with respect.*
  Is there an issue you need to discuss with your spouse

about either set of your parents? Talk about how
Exodus 20:12 and Genesis 2:24 speak into that issue.

• *Husbands: Work hard to hear your wife's heart and meet
  her needs.*
  Read John 3:16 aloud, inserting your wife's name where
  appropriate. How does that help you better appreciate
  God's love for her? How does it impact your attitude
  toward her?

• *Husbands: Be prepared to love sacrificially.*
  How do you define *sacrifice*? In what ways do you
  sacrifice and "take the middle seat" so your spouse can
  feel loved?

• *Wives: Show love and respect to your husband.*
  Offer a sincere compliment about your spouse this week
  in front of your children, your parents or siblings, or
  your friends at church, at work, or in the neighborhood.
  If possible, do it when he is there too!

• *Wives: Strike the right balance between acceptance and
  expressing your disappointment when following your
  husband's lead in an area where you disagree.*
  Submission can be a loaded term in our culture. Take
  a few minutes today to discuss what this word means
  to you. Do you each feel that the other hears your heart
  and respects your feelings? If not, godly submission
  will be tough to practice. How might you begin to
  practice submission and meeting your spouse where
  he or she is?

UNCOMMON PRAYER

Take a few minutes to discuss any praises and needs you'd like to bring to God as a couple. Then, in addition to praying about those things, use one or more of the following prayer prompts to ask God to help you rely on Scripture and on Christ to build a stronger marriage.

Praise God that He hasn't left you alone to figure out how to love each other, but that His Word offers an abundance of wisdom to learn from, promises to claim, and examples to follow.

Throughout the week, ask the Holy Spirit to remind you of passages from His Word that can breathe new hope and joy into your marriage.

Confess your need for Christ to help you show honor, respect, and grace to your in-laws, your spouse, and even yourself when you face dashed expectations or unanticipated frustrations.

Invite Jesus to be at the center of your marriage this week, filling your hearts with love for Him and each other and infusing your relationship with uncommon affection, peace, and self-sacrifice.

day 8
WHY PATIENCE PAYS OFF

CORE PRACTICE #7:
Wait on God's timing; don't try to make things happen yourself.

Wait patiently for the LORD.
  Be brave and courageous.
  Yes, wait patiently for the LORD.

—PSALM 27:14

TONY

I know the phrase "Patience is a virtue" well. I've probably heard it hundreds of times since I was young. Yet if I were judged on that quality alone, I would probably fall woefully short.

Patience is easy to recommend to other people, but not easy to apply to ourselves. When I was young I didn't exhibit a lot of patience, even though I saw my dad live it out consistently. I often wondered why he didn't always take a stand or forge ahead when I thought he should. He simply stayed the course and relied patiently on God's timing for the right moment to correct something or for the right opportunity to make a difference.

If it had been up to me, I would have been a National Football League head coach long before Rich McKay and the Glazer family offered me that opportunity with the Tampa Bay Buccaneers. I had played in the NFL and had served as an assistant coach in the NFL under the tutelage of some great head coaches—Chuck Noll, Marty Schottenheimer, and Dennis Green. I was an assistant coach for fifteen years, and during the last ten, my name was repeatedly mentioned for potential head coaching positions.

Few people saw the inner turmoil I felt while waiting for that right opening. In fact, someone looking at me from the outside might have mistakenly said that patience clearly was one of my virtues. I knew better—patience is a state of the heart, and for many of those years my heart revolved around my plan, not God's plan for me. I couldn't have claimed to be patient in those years.

I was almost ready to give up in 1993. I was the defensive coordinator for the Minnesota Vikings, in my thirteenth year as an assistant coach, and our team had the top defense in the NFL. There were seven head coaching job vacancies that year, and yet nothing happened for me.

No interest from anyone. Not even an interview! I remember telling Lauren that since it hadn't happened that year, it probably would never happen. Lauren encouraged me to be patient because God was in control. Even better, when I felt overlooked, she kept telling me that she loved me and believed in me.

My friend Tom Lamphere, the Vikings' chaplain, also gave me some terrific advice. He told me to turn my situation over to the Lord; to trust God with where He had me and with His plan for my life. In the meantime, he said, my responsibility was to be the very best I could be wherever God had me.

The next year brought the same disappointment—I learned of several head coaching openings, but none for which I was being considered. Whatever patience I had was running out.

And then God opened a door with the Tampa Bay Buccaneers. As it turned out, it was the perfect spot for me and my family at just the right time. Looking back over my NFL coaching career, I always smile as I consider God's timing. The experience I gained in so many settings as an assistant made me a better head coach. During those years as an assistant, I ended up meeting and working with many different men who would later become part of my staff. And the time I spent learning and growing—sometimes with godly patience and sometimes with forced acceptance—served me well in my thirteen years as a head coach.

Even though I retired from coaching in 2009, people still kindly say that I am young enough to coach again someday. Who says God doesn't have a sense of timing—and humor!

Adventure Application: What are you and your spouse waiting for—a new job, a baby, a home, the return of a wayward teen? In what ways are you trusting God while you wait? How might you encourage your spouse to hang in there when God doesn't seem to be moving?

day 9
ID CHECK

CORE PRACTICE #8:
Find your identity in Christ, not in the world.

....

This means that anyone who belongs to Christ has become a new person.
The old life is gone; a new life has begun! —2 CORINTHIANS 5:17

Lauren

It's fun now, these many years after Tony was dismissed from the Bucs' head coaching job, to watch people's reactions when our family goes out in public in Tampa. Our children are always mildly amused when they overhear someone whisper, "That's Tony Dungy!" as we walk by. All of the children now know that Tony was once the head coach for the Tampa Bay Buccaneers, but the youngest boys don't understand why complete strangers seem to know their dad. They don't yet appreciate the visibility a head coach in the National Football League can have.

When we have a chance to talk with the people who stop to greet us, they seem to fondly remember our days with the Buccaneers. However, our younger children don't understand that not everyone had a favorable impression of Tony during his tenure as the head football coach. The older children no doubt remember the boos rising up from the crowd when the team didn't play well or meet expectations in any particular year.

Most Tampa football fans back then—and now—know Tony only as the Bucs' coach. To them, that's his identity. Other people may remember Tony as the head football coach with the Indianapolis Colts from 2002 through 2008. Still others may recognize him in his current role with NBC as studio color analyst along with Rodney Harrison, Dan Patrick, and so many other talented people on *Football Night in America*. Some may even know me as a spokesperson for iMom, as a volunteer who reads in schools for the Dungy Family Foundation, or as the woman who often speaks on adoptions. Those are our public "identities."

But those roles are not where our true selves really lie. Identity might be defined as "the distinguishing character or personality of a person."[3] Our roles do not define who we *are*. That's a lesson we try to teach our children as well. Those roles are certainly fun, and it's a privilege to work with great people who have become dear friends, but they are not the essence of who we are.

Our entire family enjoyed the cheers that always came with a Buccaneers' or Colts' victory. The boos, on the other hand, were never pleasant to hear. But we weren't swayed by them and didn't make impulsive decisions because of them. Our identity, then and now, is found in Christ. Tony and I want to be known for making decisions that come out of our relationship with Him. That is why the applause or criticism from the world never guided our choices or direction. It still doesn't.

Our relationship with Christ—His grace, loving correction, and guidance for every step we take and every fork in the road we encounter—is what shapes our identity. And it's how we live in that relationship, and what we do with and for Him that counts, both now and eternally.

That's what we try to share with our children, at some level, whenever the whispers or pointing fingers come from the outside.

Adventure Application: If you polled your neighbors, friends, and coworkers, what do you think they'd say you're known for—your immaculate yard, your sports-crazy kids, your jobs, or your roles at church? How likely is it that they would ID you as a Christ follower?

day 10
LESSONS FOR MOM—
AND MR. MOM

CORE PRACTICE #9:
Look to God as the source for all the stamina and patience you need.

....

*I know how to live on almost nothing or with everything. I have
learned the secret of living in every situation, whether it is with a full
stomach or empty, with plenty or little. For I can do everything through
Christ, who gives me strength.* —PHILIPPIANS 4:12-13

TONY

I don't know how Lauren accomplishes all that she does at home.
I am continually amazed by her many abilities and stamina,
which enable her to get through everything and come out on
the other side of each day with a smile and sense of satisfaction.
A lesser person—me, for example—might actually consider not
even getting out of bed on a few of those days.

This became apparent to me not too long ago. I had caught
glimpses of it before, but when I was coaching, I didn't often
experience Lauren's daytime routine firsthand. Now, in my current role as a studio analyst with NBC Sports, I have some time
during the week, even during football season, to help out (or
at least try to).

Our young teenage son Jordan, whose congenital insensitivity to pain has caused him to have frequent fractures and other
injuries, is a trouper. Recently he had to undergo a surgical
procedure in New York, where he had to be hospitalized for
four days. Lauren traveled with Jordan and remained with him
at the hospital.

I was Mr. Mom to our other children who were at home, where I was tasked with picking up Lauren's mantle of daily responsibilities and making sure things continued to run smoothly. Although I knew there would be quite a bit to do, I felt reasonably confident that with all of my life experiences, both personally and professionally, I would be fine.

It didn't take me long—a few hours actually—to realize that I had drastically underestimated the task before me and over-estimated my abilities to handle these responsibilities with the care, wisdom, patience, and energy required. Not only was I the scheduler and chauffeur, making sure everyone was where they were supposed to be when they were supposed to be there, but I also needed to fix the meals and help the younger children dress. I had to monitor and assist with homework—at least when I was competent enough to do so. And then there was the role of mediator over regular sibling disagreements. I had to juggle all this while holding our two youngest children, who always wanted to be held by Dad.

After just one day I was completely worn out, wondering how in the world Lauren managed. I was ready to call someone to take over the next day so I could have a brief leave of absence to recover. How was she able to do this day after day? How did she summon the energy and maintain an attitude of patience while making the decisions for our children's individual and collective good, often on the fly?

Lauren does it through God's consistent presence and power within her, as well as His overarching peace, which is always greater than whatever she faces. Lauren knows that what she does is all about what God is doing with and through her in the context of those responsibilities. She knows that not only is He walking with her and often talking her through many of these moments, but that He is also using all of her circumstances to grow her more into the woman He created her to be.

To Lauren, whatever she faces is not about her. It's all about God working through her. She knows that her focus cannot be on herself and what is happening or will happen throughout the day, but on Him and what He is doing and will do for her—no matter what she faces.

With a similar focus, maybe I will do better the next time I get a chance to be Mr. Mom!

Adventure Application: Where do you need to redirect your focus from your own efforts, abilities, and shortcomings to God and His strength and power? How can you also encourage your spouse to look to the Lord for his or her needs?

day 11
RESTING IN GOD'S PROMISES

CORE PRACTICE #10:
Cling to each other and to God's promises that
He is always with you when you face hard times.

....

Trust in the LORD and do good.
  Then you will live safely in the land and prosper.
Take delight in the LORD,
  and he will give you your heart's desires.
Commit everything you do to the LORD.
  Trust him, and he will help you.
He will make your innocence radiate like the dawn,
  and the justice of your cause will shine like the noonday sun.

—PSALM 37:3-6

TONY

If someone in our family is going through a difficult moment, we all tend to share in it, doing our best to buoy the person who is struggling. That's how it always works.

January 2002 was such a time. I lost my mother just after the beginning of the new year. My mom was a schoolteacher and a stickler for studying, writing well, and encouraging her kids and her students to do the best we could in everything we set our hands and minds to do. As you would expect, losing her left a void in my life that I felt for some time thereafter, and even today.

Later that month I was fired from my position as head coach of the Tampa Bay Buccaneers. It came after being with the organization for six years, and there was a lot of speculation in the media about what might happen after that season. I felt we'd had remarkable success. The team had done a lot to stabilize the franchise and to set it on a long-term course for sustainable success. We just couldn't seem to get far enough into the playoffs and failed to reach that ultimate goal, the Super Bowl.

I remember reflecting on that period of my life for quite a while as I wrote *Quiet Strength*. I didn't become absorbed in those painful moments, but instead I remember spending some time thinking about what God had done and what He would be doing in the future in our lives.

I recalled that during those difficult days, I needed those closest and most important to me to be around me. Of course, that included Lauren, and as expected, she was my chief comforter and encourager. But she was also my number one challenger, not allowing me to wallow in feeling sorry for myself but reminding me to look to the Lord whenever I was discouraged. Also, she encouraged me to remember that God hadn't gone anywhere, and that when He closed one door in life, He was already making certain that another would open.

Lauren and I were regularly drawn back to promises of His protection, presence, and plans for our lives. We remembered such assurances as those in Jeremiah 29:11: "'For I know the plans I have for you,'" says the Lord. "'They are plans for good and not for disaster, to give you a future and a hope.'" Although Lauren helped keep me grounded in what we truly believed about God, she also realized that a part of me was hurt and needed some time to heal. So she made sure to stay close, to affirm me in many other ways, and simply to make sure I knew she loved me.

Together we focused on promises such as those expressed in the verses of today's Scripture passage, trusting in the Lord and taking delight in Him and His ways. We believed that when we did that, He would give us the desires of our hearts—in His time and aligned with His will. We committed everything to the Lord—our hurts, needs, hopes, family, and lives—because He, and He alone, could be trusted with all of that and more.

Not only did we make it through those tough times, as He knew we would, we began to thrive once again. Turn to Him and He will do the same for you, no matter what you face.

Adventure Application: Today's passage from Psalm 37 is worth committing to memory—or at least marking in your Bible so you can read it aloud when you're particularly discouraged. Take a few moments, too, to discuss what this Scripture means for you as a couple today.

day 12
MORE THAN ONE WAY TO GROW A FAMILY

CORE PRACTICE #11:
Prepare your mind and heart so you are ready
for the opportunities God brings to you.

How joyful are those who fear the LORD—
all who follow his ways!
You will enjoy the fruit of your labor.
How joyful and prosperous you will be!
Your wife will be like a fruitful grapevine,
flourishing within your home.
Your children will be like vigorous young olive trees
as they sit around your table.
That is the LORD's blessing
for those who fear him.

—PSALM 128:1-4

Lauren

I always wanted a big family. Tony wanted a big family as well. It's just that my definition and his definition of *big*—let's say they might have been a *little* different.

Don't get me wrong; Tony dearly loves all our children and is an incredible, hands-on, involved father. But he grew up with three siblings, and I think when we first talked about having children, he was probably thinking that four kids would be a nice, round number.

I grew up with four siblings and many more cousins within my extended family. I always considered our large family to be a gift from God. As a result, after Tony and I got married, I was always praying for and looking forward to having a large family full of children of our own.

God answered my prayers, but in His own divine way and perfect timing.

When we married, I was a sixth-grade teacher and never lacked for a classroom of children to love, nurture, and encourage. I learned to look for the opportunities God gave me to make a difference in my students' lives, to share the love of God with each of them, and to help them find their own sense of self-worth. Tony, of course, had his own "boys" to mentor—the players he was coaching.

Little did we know as a newly married couple what else God had in mind for us. Perhaps Tony should have seen a glimpse when we got a dog . . . and then another . . . and then another! One quickly turned into three. Of course, since we didn't have children at that time, maybe he didn't have reason to see the parallel between a houseful of dogs and my vision of a big family.

Even as newlyweds, we'd always had a soft spot in our hearts for those who were down on their luck and needed uplifting in life. After all, God models such care for us all through His Word. So when God provided opportunities for us to help children through the local foster care agency in Pittsburgh, we took them. Today we thank God for giving us the opportunity to have nurtured more than twenty-five foster children.

As we look back, we realize that if our hearts and minds had been set just on having children of our own, we might have missed some of these opportunities to be instruments of God's love through the years. But of course, over time God also blessed us with nine children of our own. We have the big family we always wanted—maybe bigger than Tony envisioned, but just perfect for us.

Do I still believe a big family is a blessing? You bet. And only God knew how best to prepare us for His gift!

Adventure Application: Instead of focusing on something you want God to do for you, open your mind wide to all the possibilities that God may have planned for you this very day. Is there a door of opportunity you have closed that God's been looking to reopen? Pray for such an opening—and for an open heart to walk through it in faith.

day 13

GOD'S GLORY AND GRACE IN OUR TROUBLES

CORE PRACTICE #12:
Run to God rather than from Him when troubles come.

....

But as for me, I will sing about your power.
  Each morning I will sing with joy about your unfailing love.
For you have been my refuge,
  a place of safety when I am in distress.

—PSALM 59:16

TONY

I suppose I have been as guilty of it as anyone else has through the years—looking at other people's lives and seeing only the good things without realizing the heartache and pain that is there, often just under the surface.

So I guess I should understand when people tend to look at our lives that way. They see Lauren and me as well-paid, highly visible people involved in professional sports. They know I work with football players who are talked about on every sports show across the nation. Most folks probably assume that our world is glamorous and full of fun, with very few problems.

I would understand if someone looked at our thirty-one years of marriage and focused on all the good things that have happened to us. The reality is that we *have* been blessed, but not always in the way those looking at us from the outside would understand.

In the midst of the wonderful moments, there have been times of incredible heartache, pain, and disappointment that we weren't sure we could overcome. We're just like everyone else.

We've had to deal with health scares, being fired from a job, and the indescribable pain of losing a child. Even in the most excruciating moments, we have felt God's presence. He's always been a refuge and a source of strength. In those tough times, we always reached a place of assurance by turning to Him in prayer.

The truth of Paul's words in Romans 8:28 has been a source of comfort for us time and again: "And we know that God causes everything to work together for the good of those who love God and are called according to his purpose for them."

Think about that for a moment. *In the midst of whatever you face—God is weaving it all together for your good and His glory.* In that promise you, too, can find divine assurance, rest, and peace.

When our son Jamie died, we wondered what good could possibly come from it. Eight years later, while on the book promotional tour for *Uncommon Marriage* in Indianapolis, a Delta ticket agent at the airport told us how much we had helped her during a tough period in her life. Her family had lost everything in a house fire, and she was mad at God. Then she read our story of losing Jamie. When she realized that we were still trying to honor the Lord in the midst of our grief and shock, her outlook on her own situation changed.

I remember her telling us, "I had only lost possessions. You guys had lost a life. At that point I knew I had to get up and come back to God." Her story gave us a glimpse of how God uses even tragic situations for His glory.

Adventure Application: In what area of your life have you been running away from God, not allowing Him to help you? Turn it over to Him, trusting Him today to begin to assist you with whatever it is. He will.

day 14

PRINCIPLE 1
LOOK TO THE BIBLE AS YOUR GUIDEBOOK AND TO CHRIST AS YOUR LIVING EXAMPLE.

UNCOMMON WISDOM

Oh, the joys of those who do not
  follow the advice of the wicked,
  or stand around with sinners,
  or join in with mockers.
But they delight in the law of the LORD,
  meditating on it day and night.
They are like trees planted along the riverbank,
  bearing fruit each season.
Their leaves never wither,
  and they prosper in all they do.

—PSALM 1:1-3

UNCOMMON PRACTICE

Take a few moments to select one of this week's practices to explore further. The related Adventure Application appears just below each practice. If you'd prefer to come up with a different way of living out that practice this week, feel free to discuss what that might look like.

- *Wait on God's timing; don't try to make things happen yourself.*
  What are you and your spouse waiting for—a new job, a baby, a home, the return of a wayward teen? In what

ways are you trusting God while you wait? How might
you encourage your spouse to hang in there when God
doesn't seem to be moving?

- *Find your identity in Christ, not in the world.*
  If you polled your neighbors, friends, and coworkers,
  what do you think they'd say you're known for—your
  immaculate yard, your sports-crazy kids, your jobs, or
  your roles at church? How likely is it that they would ID
  you as a Christ follower?

- *Look to God as the source for all the stamina and
  patience you need.*
  Where do you need to redirect your focus from your
  own efforts, abilities, and shortcomings to God and
  His strength and power? How can you encourage your
  spouse to look to the Lord for his or her needs too?

- *Cling to each other and to God's promises that He is
  always with you when you face hard times.*
  Psalm 37:3-6 is worth committing to memory—or at
  least marking in your Bible so you can read it aloud
  when you're particularly discouraged. Take a few
  moments, too, to discuss what this Scripture means for
  you as a couple today.

- *Prepare your mind and heart so you are ready for the
  opportunities God brings to you.*
  Instead of focusing on something you want God to do
  for you, open your mind wide to all the possibilities that
  God may have planned for you this very day. Is there
  a door of opportunity you have closed that God's been

looking to reopen? Pray for such an opening—and for an open heart to walk through it in faith.

- *Run to God rather than from Him when troubles come.* In what area of your life have you been running away from God, not allowing Him to help you? Turn it over to Him, trusting Him today to begin to assist you with whatever it is. He will.

UNCOMMON PRAYER

Take a few minutes to discuss any praises and needs you'd like to bring to God as a couple. Then, in addition to praying about those things together, use one or more of the following prayer prompts to ask God to help you rely on Scripture and on Christ to build a stronger marriage.

Praise God that His wisdom is absolute, His timing is perfect, His promises are trustworthy, and His grace is boundless.

As you look ahead to your plans and commitments for the coming week, ask the Holy Spirit to give you the love, joy, peace, patience, kindness, goodness, faithfulness, gentleness, or self-control you will need.[4]

Ask the Lord to give you His perspective on the people and opportunities you encounter this week.

day 15

TALK ISN'T ALWAYS CHEAP

CORE PRACTICE #13:
Communicate about spiritual matters—which should be the number one priority of your life.

....

Let your conversation be gracious and attractive so that you will have the right response for everyone. —COLOSSIANS 4:6

Lauren

I have a friend who is a gifted facilitator of group conversations. He puts people at ease, whether he's leading discussions between couples, members of sports teams, small group Bible studies, church or business committees, or in larger gatherings. His key to success is evident in the way he treats and responds to others: He strongly believes that everyone has something to share and should have the opportunity to do so, no matter how big the setting.

No matter what they say or how silly or inappropriate their comments may seem at the time, he makes everyone who speaks feel affirmed simply for taking the risk to communicate their feelings to others. As a result, learning takes place, conflict is lessened, team unity is enhanced, and productivity is increased.

Webster's New World Dictionary of the American Language, College Edition, defines *communication* as: "giving, or giving and receiving, of information, signals, or messages by talk, gestures, writing, etc." Between individuals, communication takes many forms, as it does between Tony and me. We have learned not only what the spoken words from each other usually mean, but we have learned to decipher the nuances in the tone or manner in which they are delivered. We have learned what certain facial expressions, hand signals, and body mannerisms mean. That's been especially true for me, since Tony didn't talk much in the early years! Together our words and body language allow us to communicate effectively. Of course, that's only because we have spent years learning the language between us.

Communication between God and humans requires the same discipline. It takes practice; it takes spending time in the presence of the living God to be able to learn to communicate effectively with Him. When you do this consistently, you will you feel as though you are connecting to that divine source of power for your life.

One way to draw closer to God is through regular daily prayer. We learn to hear from and speak with God as we study His Word. We become better communicators when we talk with one another about something God has revealed to us through prayer, His Word, or a wise teacher. Conversing with God and then telling others about the Lord and what He is trying to show us is one of the most life-changing disciplines in which we can engage.

It should come as no surprise that Tony and I enjoyed attending church together on Sundays when we were dating. Afterward, we would go out to lunch and spend hours discussing the sermon and other aspects of the worship service. "What did you get out of that?" "What do you think the pastor meant when he said . . . ?" "What point do you think he was trying to make with that story about the little girl?"

As our conversation heated up, our half-eaten food grew colder by the minute. When we engaged in this give-and-take, we often found we were on the same page with what we heard. But sometimes we had each pulled something much different from the message. That was when we realized how God used both of us to expand the point He was trying to pass along to the other person through that day's message. So while I may never be as gifted a facilitator as my friend, I hope I never stop trying to better communicate with Tony, those around me, and God.

Adventure Application: Choose one way to grow in your communication with each other and with God this week. You might decide to spend a few minutes together praising God or asking for His direction in a certain area of your life. Or you might discuss a sermon, Scripture passage, or book you're reading over lunch some day this week.

day 16
GROUP DYNAMICS

CORE PRACTICE #14: Look for opportunities to study the Bible with your spouse and/or in a small group.

....

One day as he saw the crowds gathering, Jesus went up on the mountainside and sat down. His disciples gathered around him, and he began to teach them. . . . When Jesus had finished saying these things, the crowds were amazed at his teaching, for he taught with real authority—quite unlike their teachers of religious law. —MATTHEW 5:1-2; 7:28-29

TONY

About five years ago, John and Celeste Salgado, friends of ours from church, began talking about starting a couple's Bible study. Lauren and I decided to give the small group a try.

I can't think of a better example of Christ followers learning Kingdom principles in a small-group setting than in the way that Jesus taught His own "small group" of disciples. Christ chose to pour all the knowledge and wisdom of His Father and His plans for His Kingdom into these twelve men.

After mentoring them, the apostle Luke says Jesus "sent them out to tell everyone about the Kingdom of God and to heal the sick" (Luke 9:2). Yet He also ensured that the group had time for rest: "When the apostles returned, they told Jesus everything they had done. Then he slipped quietly away with them toward the town of Bethsaida" (v. 10). As the Master Teacher painstakingly taught, directed, encouraged, and sent out His disciples—right there in that small-group setting—He was laying the foundation for a movement that would change the world.

As for the Salgados and our small group, we decided to meet

on Thursday evenings and adopted a DVD series of Bible studies for our initial lesson plans. All the couples took turns preparing food and serving the meal to our small group. Others took the responsibility of arranging for an on-site babysitter to care for our younger children. Whenever other needs become apparent, group members stepped forward to help out.

The people in our small group have changed through the years because of unavoidable scheduling conflicts and moves out of the area, but the group has consistently ranged in size from eight to twelve couples. We have covered great biblical material and teachings on love; improving our marriages around the cornerstone of Christ; consistent and loving parenting; and recognizing, dealing with, and seeking protection from spiritual warfare. We have also participated together in a lot of social activities—nights out, 5K runs for worthwhile causes, and a number of holiday parties and other get-togethers. As a result we have grown, not only in our walk of faith, but also in a closer relationship with one another.

A natural, obvious (as we look back), but unintended consequence of growing closer has been that we've become a valuable, trusted, and indispensable support system for one another—spiritually, emotionally, educationally, and physically. But more than that, our marriages have grown stronger because of the loving and positive influence we have had on one another.

Adventure Application: If you are part of a couples' small group, how is it helping you grow? If it isn't, what might your group learn from the example of Christ and His disciples? If you're not in a group, check with your church about couples' small groups. While joining a group may seem risky, it's a great way to grow close to Christ while gaining a support system.

day 17
FIRST THINGS FIRST

CORE PRACTICE #15:
Accept that the time and place where you connect spiritually as a couple may need to change along with the seasons of your marriage.

One day soon afterward Jesus went up on a mountain to pray, and he prayed to God all night. —LUKE 6:12

Lauren

Jesus prayed a lot. A whole lot.

And He prayed in a number of different places—on the mountain, in the desert, in an upper room (giving thanks!), and in a garden. He sought out those moments because they were moments when He could be alone with the one person He loved most—His Father.

You might consider your life hectic, but consider how hard it was for Jesus and His disciples to find any time for prayer and refreshment:

> Jesus said, "Let's go off by ourselves to a quiet place and rest awhile." He said this because there were so many people coming and going that Jesus and his apostles didn't even have time to eat.
>
> So they left by boat for a quiet place, where they could be alone. But many people recognized them and saw them leaving, and people from many towns ran ahead along the shore and got there ahead of them. (Mark 6:31-33)

People always wanted to be with Jesus, which made it hard

for Him to be alone. But the one routine that Jesus kept was praying to His Father. He didn't just find time to spend with God; He *made* time to spend with Him.

That has seemed to be the key for Tony and me staying close spiritually—for growing in our relationship with God and together. We have to make time to spend with each other in study and prayer. It doesn't really matter when that time is, or even that it is on a regular schedule and time. But we make sure it happens at least one time each day.

When we were first married, Tony and I made worshiping and praying together part of our routine. We were in a wonderful church, Bethany Baptist in Pittsburgh, and our church attendance, Bible study, and prayer time was pretty consistent and regular. Still, the fall football season put a bit of a damper on our Sunday worship time together. Sunday was game day, and even when the team played at home, Tony was required to be at the stadium very early. So that made Wednesday evening Bible study and prayer at our church even more important for us.

Back then I was also teaching school full time and handling other outside projects. As busy as we both were, we decided we needed to find times during the mornings to study and pray together too. That was the best way we knew to invite God into our day and to encourage each other. We found that we could spend fifteen to twenty minutes very early in the morning for devotions and prayer. That worked, and for the first few years of our marriage, we were able to stick to that routine.

After we had children, we agreed that early mornings were still the best time to pray and study the Bible together. Once Tony headed into the office, particularly during football season, we knew we'd have little time together until the next morning. As I said, we joined a couple's Bible study on Thursday evenings several years ago, which became another way to connect with God and each other. We also kept and continue to keep a journal by the nightstand, which is where we jot down prayer requests that we can pray for together whenever we have a few minutes.

At times Tony and I have been concerned that we've given God the leftovers of our day. I'm sure you occasionally share that feeling. But the reality was that we also had responsibilities to many others who were counting on us to make it all work. We knew God was available anytime, so we just needed to be flexible while making sure we didn't overlook meeting regularly with each other and with Him.

What a comfort it is to know that God doesn't care what time we meet with Him—He just wants us to join Him. So whether you meet early in the morning or late at night, be sure to put first things first by purposefully agreeing on a set time to meet with God.

Adventure Application: Try to schedule at least three or four times this week that you and your spouse can spend together in devotional study and prayer. Then complement that with Sunday worship time at a Bible-teaching church of your choice.

day 18
FREE FOR THE ASKING

CORE PRACTICE #16:
Ask God to give you His infinite wisdom and to make you of one mind as you pray about decisions.

....

If you need wisdom, ask our generous God, and he will give it to you. He will not rebuke you for asking. —JAMES 1:5

TONY

In 2010, our son Eric accepted a football scholarship to the University of Oregon. Lauren and I knew we would want to be with him as much as possible while he was in college. Initially, we wanted to help Eric get settled and acclimated to his new surroundings, but we also wanted to be there to support him during the football season.

Since Eugene, Oregon, is just over three thousand miles from our home in Tampa, Lauren and I agreed it might be a good idea to buy a small house or a condominium in the area as a second home. We planned to take vacations there in the summer and spend as many football weekends in Eugene as we could each fall. That was the easy part of the decision. The hard parts were deciding which home was the right one for us and then negotiating a price consistent with our desire to be good stewards of the resources God had entrusted to our care. We would be there ten to twelve weeks of the year, and so the house didn't have to be perfect—just clean, comfortable, and ready to move into.

What's the best way for a couple to make such a major decision? This may be one of the harder processes to wrap our brains around—finding peace in decision making, especially when agreement appears to be a *long* way off. Lauren and I know through experience that such consensus isn't always easy to achieve, and often the attempt creates more tension in our marriage than we would like. But we've discovered one thing that definitely gets in the way: when we allow our base human nature to direct our steps, or when we rely on our own wisdom to make tough choices, we often get stuck.

The apostle James provides a better alternative. God is pretty clear: seek His wisdom in all matters and He will provide for you. Asking for God's direction may not be our natural inclination, but it needs to become a regular spiritual discipline in our lives.

Lauren and I did pray for direction as we began our home search. We finally narrowed the choice down to three and eventually selected the one we both liked best. When the seller wouldn't budge on the asking price, however, we wondered whether that was God's way of directing us to another choice. We continued to pray through the process and sought God's wisdom for our decision—did He want us to reconsider one of the other two homes?

After much discussion and more prayer, we finally felt that we were on the same page and had been led there by God—we were back to house number one. We had peace and felt it was a wise choice for a number of reasons: the layout, the convenient location, and the resale value of the home when Eric finished at the University of Oregon. We moved ahead with the purchase.

The wisdom of our decision was confirmed in the months that followed, and we realized God could see some advantages that we didn't know when we were moving ahead with that purchase. We soon met several Christian families in our neighborhood, and one in particular—the Cooley family—became special friends. Not only did we become extremely close, but they were kind enough to look after the house while we were back in Tampa, giving our home the care it needed and us the peace of mind we needed. Looking back, we know that this was the house God had waiting for us.

Fortunately, we were of one mind regarding this decision— the mind of God. Little did we know that He was leading us to wonderful memories of new and dear friends, great summers, and exciting fall weekends.

Adventure Application: What are you and your spouse having trouble agreeing upon today? Resolve not to talk about it any longer but instead to begin praying together about the situation, seeking God's wisdom as you pray.

day 19
DOUBLE BLESSING

CORE PRACTICE #17:
Remember that God will answer your prayers in His own timing—and in ways you might not expect.

....

She became pregnant, and she gave birth to a son for Abraham in his old age. This happened at just the time God had said it would. —GENESIS 21:2

Lauren

Think about God answering the prayers of Abraham and Sarah for a moment. If nothing else, it will give you a dramatic boost in assurance that God is powerful and He will do what He promises.

Consider this: When Sarah gave birth to Isaac, she was about ninety-one years old, and Abraham was one hundred years old. God had always planned it for that time—even when He had first promised Abram (he was still going by his given name then) a son twenty-five years before.

But by age ninety-nine, Abram seemed to have lost hope that he and his wife would ever have a child of their own. Genesis 17 tells us that the Lord appeared to him and made a covenant with him. As confirmation of His promise to give Abram a child, God told him He was changing his name to Abraham, which means "father of many." Even then, Abraham doubted that God could do what He said He would do. Just read his response when the Lord reaffirmed His promise:

> Then Abraham bowed down to the ground, but he
> laughed to himself in disbelief. "How could I become

a father at the age of 100?" he thought. "And how can Sarah have a baby when she is ninety years old?" (Genesis 17:17)

Too often you and I are like Abraham. We are the classic carriers of doubt. All of us, at some time or another, discount God's promises and power. And much to the chagrin of our Father, we often forget the times He has been faithful to us in the past.

Specifically, in my own life, I wanted the Lord to bless Tony and me with lots of children, and I especially wanted Him to give us a set of twins. Being a twin myself and coming from a large family, I often prayed for both of those blessings.

By the year 1999, after we had been married for seventeen years, Tony and I had three beautiful and wonderful children. But we still didn't have the set of twins for which I had been praying. I had quite a few years left before I caught up with Sarah, but I wasn't sure I had that kind of patience in me. I was happy but not confident my prayers had been truly answered. My specific prayers for twins had *definitely* not been answered.

Little did I know that God was not finished. Through the blessing of adoption, God gave us six more children during the next twelve years—still no twins (which was probably a relief to Tony)—but we definitely have a wonderfully large family.

And who knows? Maybe God has more in store for us. Tony is worried that, like Abraham, we might bring home another child when he is one hundred years old.

I'll keep praying. (Maybe the twins are on the way?) One thing I know for sure: God's timing is always perfect!

Adventure Application: What is it that you have been seeking? What is it that you have been praying for? Lay it before the Lord again today, but be open to His timing and His answer—it may be different from what you expect.

day 20

SEEKING GOD'S GRACE IN THE GOOD TIMES

CORE PRACTICE #18:
Continue to pray together in the good times—that's often when couples make foolish mistakes.

....

But that is the time to be careful! Beware that in your plenty you do not forget the LORD your God and disobey his commands, regulations, and decrees that I am giving you today. . . . Do not become proud at that time and forget the LORD your God, who rescued you from slavery in the land of Egypt. . . . He did all this so you would never say to yourself, "I have achieved this wealth with my own strength and energy." Remember the LORD your God. He is the one who gives you power to be successful. —DEUTERONOMY 8:11, 14, 17, 18

Lauren

When Tony was coaching, nearly everything in our lives revolved around football. The scheduling of family trips, mealtimes, weekend activities—all were done with his football games and other responsibilities in mind. And when his team was winning, everyone seemed to take these commitments in stride.

Life seemed to go more smoothly during winning streaks too: our routines at home, early morning wake-ups, breakfast and trips to school, the children's homework assignments, even the weather was better on those days. Or maybe it just seemed that way. Whatever the reason, you may be able to identify with what I'm talking about: When life is generally going well with your family's health, relationships, and income, everything seems easier to deal with, and everyone has a lighter spirit. All appears well with the world.

When we were with the Indianapolis Colts, several seasons included long winning streaks: We won thirteen in a row in 2005 and nine consecutive games in 2006. Yet those were the very times Tony and I learned we needed to be on guard—and on our knees before God. We thanked Him for the good times and for the things that had come to pass as we had hoped. But we sought continued protection as well. We also prayed as a way to remind ourselves that all the good that was happening was due to God. We needed Him to help guard us against the onset of pride. After all, He deserves the credit, not us.

When things seem to be going well, we can all fall into the trap of thinking it's because of our own doing. Whether we want to admit it or not, in the good times we tend to become complacent and forget who got us there—God. We have no problem seeking Him, finding Him, and appealing for His help when we are in a pit of despair. But we need to seek His help when we are in the rarified air of good times as well. It's then we most need to ask for His perspective, not ours, and to remember that He is due our thanks. Then we can use those times of plenty for the good of others and to glorify Him.

Adventure Application: If you were to picture a mountain, would you describe yourself as being at its summit, enjoying fresh air and a spectacular view, or at the base, with your view so obscured by fog that it's difficult to even see the top? Either way, spend some time seeking God in prayer today. Be sure to thank Him, to appeal to Him for His perspective, and to remember that all you are and have is a result of His graciousness to you.

day 21

PRINCIPLE 2
STAY IN SYNC SPIRITUALLY.

UNCOMMON WISDOM

Pray in the Spirit at all times and on every occasion. Stay alert and be persistent in your prayers for all believers everywhere. —EPHESIANS 6:18

UNCOMMON PRACTICE

Take a few moments to select one of this week's practices to explore further. The related Adventure Application appears just below each practice. If you'd prefer to come up with a different way of living out that practice this week, feel free to discuss what that might look like.

- *Communicate about spiritual matters—which should be the number one priority of your life.*
  Choose one way to grow in your communication with each other and with God this week. You might decide to spend a few minutes together praising God or asking for His direction in a certain area of your life. Or you might discuss a sermon, Scripture passage, or book you're reading over lunch some day this week.

- *Look for opportunities to study the Bible with your spouse and/or in a small group.*
  If you are part of a couples' small group, how is it helping you grow? If it isn't, what might your group learn from the example of Christ and His disciples? If you're not in a group, check with your church about

couples' small groups. While joining a group may seem risky, it's a great way to grow close to Christ while gaining a support system.

- *Accept that the time and place where you connect spiritually as a couple may need to change along with the seasons of your marriage.*
  Try to schedule at least three or four times this week that you and your spouse can spend together in devotional study and prayer. Then complement that with Sunday worship time at a Bible-teaching church of your choice.

- *Ask God to give you His infinite wisdom and to make you of one mind as you pray about decisions.*
  What are you and your spouse having trouble agreeing upon today? Resolve not to talk about it any longer but instead to begin praying together about the situation, seeking God's wisdom as you pray.

- *Remember that God will answer your prayers in His own timing—and in ways you might not expect.*
  What is it that you have been seeking? What is it that you have been praying for? Lay it before the Lord again today, but be open to His timing and His answer—it may be different from what you expect.

- *Continue to pray together in the good times—that's often when couples make foolish mistakes.*
  If you were to picture a mountain, would you describe yourselves as being at its summit, enjoying fresh air and a spectacular view, or at the base, with your view so obscured by fog that it's difficult to even see the top? Either way, spend some time seeking God in prayer

today. Be sure to thank Him, to appeal to Him for His perspective, and to remember that all you are and have is a result of His graciousness to you.

UNCOMMON PRAYER

Take a few minutes to discuss any praises and needs you'd like to bring to God as a couple. Then, in addition to praying about those things together, use one or more of the following prayer prompts to ask God to help you stay in sync spiritually.

Praise God for the gifts of His Word and of prayer, evidence that He loves you and wants a continual relationship with you.

Confess any unresolved frustration or bitterness between the two of you that has developed because of trying circumstances or difficult decision making.

Ask the Holy Spirit to guide you in your prayers for each member of your family, for your future, and for your faith.

Ask the Lord to give you His perspective on your desires and dreams.

day 22

BECAUSE YOU DON'T HAVE ALL THE ANSWERS

CORE PRACTICE #19:
Consider the input and wisdom of others when making decisions.

A wise man will hear and increase in learning, and a man of understanding will acquire wise counsel. —PROVERBS 1:5, NASB

Lauren

Jerry Clower was one of the funniest and most animated comedians in recent memory—and his jokes were clean! He was a follower of Christ who died in 1998, and he probably has God in stitches with a steady barrage of good jokes, punctuated with his famous laugh.

When speaking about serious matters, Jerry often shared a series of questions to help people who were trying to make a difficult decision. His formula can help all of us determine if we are moving in the right direction or if, as Jerry used to say, we are "fixin' to mess up."

When faced with a big decision, he suggested we ask these four questions:

1. *Will God be pleased if I decide to do this thing?*
2. *Is it okay with me for others to see me doing it?*
3. *Will it hurt anyone?*
4. *How many people have I sought approval from to do it?*

These are sound principles to apply to any decision. The fourth question deserves further discussion because we can all identify with that one. When we're trying to make a decision, we may keep asking anyone with a pulse what they think we should do. Sometimes that's a dead giveaway that we're "fixin' to mess up." And while it's a good idea to seek many counselors, I've found it's a better idea to seek Christian counsel.

Yet if we ask, not because we're looking for someone to affirm what we want to do but because we are honestly seeking the Lord's direction, we're on the right track. In today's Scripture passage, King Solomon tells us that a seeker with that attitude will "increase in learning" and "acquire wise counsel." Many godly people can provide the answers we need, and they can be trusted to advise us with our best interests in mind.

Charla and Armando Hernandez have become good friends of ours through our small group Bible study. Armando is an electrical contractor with a lot of experience with housing and residential construction. Charla has a great eye for decorating. She knows how to create an interior design that reflects the individual tastes and personality of the homeowner.

So it was very natural, as well as wise and right, to ask them their opinion when we were remodeling our home. Tony and I had a pretty good idea of what we wanted to do and why, but it was so comforting to have this couple who knew quite a bit more than we did to inform and guide us in the process. Many times during the remodeling, they told us to go with what we liked, but on other occasions they pointed out factors we would never have considered. Our home and family life are proof that we can all benefit from the wisdom and experience of "wise counsel."

Adventure Application: What decision do you or your family need to make? Review Jerry Clower's four questions for decision making, and then discuss how you might answer them in light of the options you are considering.

day 23
CHURCH SURVEY

CORE PRACTICE #20: Plug into a church that offers solid biblical teaching and where you feel at home.

....

All the believers devoted themselves to the apostles' teaching, and to fellowship, and to sharing in meals (including the Lord's Supper), and to prayer. A deep sense of awe came over them all, and the apostles performed many miraculous signs and wonders. . . . They worshiped together at the Temple each day, met in homes for the Lord's Supper, and shared their meals with great joy and generosity—all the while praising God and enjoying the goodwill of all the people. And each day the Lord added to their fellowship those who were being saved. —ACTS 2:42-43, 46-47

TONY

Recent studies on church membership and attendance are uncovering some alarming trends. Fewer and fewer people attend church these days—probably not a surprise to you.

For those who go to church regularly, fewer are sticking with one church. People don't seem to be willing to stay at one church anymore, or even in one particular denomination, simply because their parents belonged to it. They're not even content staying in churches where they have worshiped for years if the needs of their family start to change.

And that's okay, as long as they're focused on the right reasons for moving.

Our family has actually changed churches three times during the seventeen years we have lived in Tampa. Each church was solid in the teaching of the Word, and each provided an edifying worship experience. There was nothing *wrong* with any of the churches, nor did anything happen to make us leave them. There was no change in leadership, no scandal, no problem of any kind. We loved the pastors and had many great friends in each congregation. We still do.

The impetus for each move was the changing dynamic of our growing family. Over the years we found ourselves with children of different ages and in different stages of their spiritual development. We have moved to another church when we knew a certain type of youth program would help our children grow best. But all the churches we have attended have three things in common: sound biblical teaching, corporate worship services that provide the opportunity to praise God, and friendly congregations.

Another thing these churches had in common? We felt as if we were home. In fact, when we teamed up with Tyndale, our publisher, to produce a simulcast shortly after the release of our book *Uncommon Marriage*, we decided to hold it at Grace Family Church, our own body of believers. We knew there was no place we'd rather share some of the lessons we've learned about building an uncommon marriage since many of the people who filled the auditorium that day were church family. Nor was there a worship team we'd rather have help us prepare and center our hearts on God before Lauren and I spoke.

But as great as it is to feel comfortable at church, that isn't the most important aspect. The teaching has to be biblical. Churches should never compromise on what Scripture says.

So wherever God happens to place you, seek a church family where teaching the Word of God is of paramount importance, where the worship of God is taken seriously, and where the people encourage one another as they grow together.

Adventure Application: Is your church meeting your family's needs at this stage? If so, that's great. If not, what should you do?

day 24
LIVING EXAMPLES

CORE PRACTICE #21:
Seek out an older couple who can model a strong marriage and family life.

....

Teach the older men to exercise self-control, to be worthy of respect, and to live wisely. They must have sound faith and be filled with love and patience.

Similarly, teach the older women to live in a way that honors God. . . . These older women must train the younger women to love their husbands and their children, to live wisely and be pure, to work in their homes, to do good, and to be submissive to their husbands. —TITUS 2:2-5

Lauren

Tony and I discovered early on that we needed to find a married couple whom we could trust, watch, and lean on for help as we began our life together. We both had the Christlike examples of our parents, who were always available for us. But we knew we also needed a Christian couple outside of our family who could bring a different perspective to our lives and marriage.

Mike and Barb Cephas, we were to find out, were that perfect couple for us. They were a deacon and deaconess at our church, Bethany Baptist in Pittsburgh. When we met them, they were raising their five children. Both Mike and Barb had strong biblical knowledge gained through years of study. They also allowed us to see the everyday side of their lives within a strong, growing family.

Mike and Barb not only were always available to counsel us, but they provided an incredible role model for Tony and me in our respective roles as husband and wife, and later as parents. Their input and time helped us grow in our faith, and often they were just the examples we needed to make the best decisions for our marriage and family. Just like in Titus 2, where the apostle Paul challenged older men and women to serve as godly examples, Mike and Barb showed us how to "live wisely" and honor each other.

Of course, the classic example of a mentor is Paul himself. He was a role model to young Timothy and others with whom he spent time. But as we can see from his thirteen letters in the New Testament, written to various groups of believers, he considered himself to be a mentor to everyone who would listen to him. He always desired to share with others about the life that Christ wanted him to live.

Like Mike and Barb Cephas, we have a wealth of life experiences that open a door for us to speak into the lives of others. It's not just pastors, teachers, or coaches who can become mentors. We can serve as examples and sounding boards with our spouses, children, friends, and coworkers.

We may even become lifelong friends with those we mentor, as the Cephases have been to us. When we met Mike and Barb, they were the ones with the big family. We didn't have children yet, and we loved going to their house to enjoy their kids. These days they are empty nesters, and with our large family, all the energy is in our house. They miss that high-energy family atmosphere, so they love coming to Tampa to visit us!

Adventure Application: Do you know a godly older couple to whom you can look for mentoring, wisdom, and guidance? Be sure to spend time with them. If you don't have such a couple in your life, try to identify one who could serve in that role. Take the first step to get to know them better this week.

day 25
BEST INTEREST IN MIND

CORE PRACTICE #22:
Be open to the possibility that the Lord is speaking to you through the input of your spouse.

....

Get all the advice and instruction you can, so you will be wise the rest of your life. You can make many plans, but the LORD's purpose will prevail. —PROVERBS 19:20-21

TONY

In some ways, baring my soul—or some of it, anyway—through writing books these last few years has been therapeutic. In addition to sharing some of my thoughts, I've discovered and admitted some of my shortcomings.

One confession I need to make is that I'm not sure I weighed Lauren's advice heavily enough in the first years of our marriage. Don't get me wrong—I always shared with Lauren what was going on, and I sought her input. I also talked with and asked for counsel from other friends.

All of which is okay, except that early on I didn't fully appreciate that Lauren's advice was usually the best, and most often the advice that would lead to the best result. I don't think I realized that Lauren really knew me better than anyone and understood what would ultimately be the most beneficial for me—and for us. The other point I finally learned was that her wisdom was not only grounded in God's Word, but that she always had my best interest at heart. No agendas other than those two—God's Word and my best interest—controlled her advice for me. At the same time, she brought a different perspective and discernment than mine.

So when coaching opportunities were presented, that's what she considered when thinking about and discussing the decision with me. In addition, Lauren always made clear that she would back me on any move that we could make work for us as a family.

After supporting me and my career for so long, Lauren began discussing one of her desires with me. Through the years Lauren and I had provided a foster home for a number of children. In 2000, those experiences and the adoption of a young boy by one of my assistant coaches—as a single parent—led Lauren to talking with me about adopting a child. I wasn't as sure as Lauren about doing that. I wasn't against adopting, but I needed some time to consider the possibility. At forty-five, I wondered if I was ready to bring another baby into our home. Not only that, but as a head coach, I had many responsibilities. We talked about it a good deal and prayed as we sought to clearly determine whether or not this was God's will for us.

When I told Lauren I wasn't sure it was the right time to adopt, she gently asked me, "Will there ever be a right time?" She pointed out that the need for adoptive parents was great, that we had the resources to commit to another child, and that we certainly had a loving home and family that could welcome a new member.

In the end, Lauren's position prevailed. And she was right. Since then, we have adopted six children. Looking back, it was clear that the Lord spoke through Lauren, and I am glad that I was listening.

Adventure Application: How can you do a better job of tuning in to your spouse and really listening to what he or she has to say? Remember that God may be sharing something He wants you to hear through him or her.

day 26
A WORD WORTH SHARING

CORE PRACTICE #23:
Share with each other the lessons you learn as you study the Bible.

··

Such things were written in the Scriptures long ago to teach us. And the Scriptures give us hope and encouragement as we wait patiently for God's promises to be fulfilled. —ROMANS 15:4

Lauren

Our family's move to Minnesota was rough on me because I had to leave a community I'd grown to love in Kansas City. I'm naturally a positive person, but for the first time in my life, I had to fight a near-daily battle against discouragement. Thankfully, I began attending a Bible Study Fellowship group, which helped me see that God was at work—even during the brutally cold winters of Minnesota.

In fact, I was so full of enthusiasm about the study and the teachings that I would often drive to Tony's office right after my class, and over lunch I would share what I had learned that week. I was so on fire about Bible Study Fellowship that it caused a fire to spark within Tony as well. I think he realized he needed to learn more and to grow spiritually, just as he was growing as a football coach.

Largely due to my enthusiasm, Tony signed up for the men's Bible Study Fellowship class that was held on Monday nights. We enjoyed going over the same material and learning some of the same lessons. The conversation during our lunches after my BSF class became even richer!

Today Tony and I do a devotional study together in the

mornings. Not only is it a great way for us to study the Word on a regular basis, but by doing it together, we can continue to help each other grow and apply the lessons we learn as individuals, as well as in our marriage and in our home.

Of course, Tony and I also often hear the same sermons and the same devotionals, and we participate in many of the same prayer services. At times we take away the same thoughts and reactions, and we sense that we are in step with what we have heard and experienced. At other times we draw slightly different, or sometimes *completely* different, pictures from what we have heard.

That's not a bad thing. When our reactions differ, I find it helpful to hear how Tony interpreted what we read or heard. It helps me look at things more deeply and to try to grasp what God may be trying to tell me, or more important, what He may be trying to do with me. Often, it causes me to examine God's Word in a way I wouldn't have seen without Tony's thoughts.

All too often, however, we don't discuss what we've been learning. Either we are geographically apart or things get hectic; it happens to everyone. Tony and I try to remember, however, that God really does require mutual accountability from us. He wants us to continually discuss with each other what we learn from His Word—whenever and wherever that occurs.

So we do our best to find the time. We remember how those lunch discussions in Minnesota helped preserve our marriage, and we know God's Word remains the center that can help us become stronger even today.

Adventure Application: Look to share at least one thing with your spouse each day this week that you learn in your private Scripture reading, devotional reading, or in a Bible study elsewhere. Encourage your spouse to add his or her insights to the discussion. You both will be doubly blessed.

day 27
SEEING THROUGH
A KNOTHOLE

CORE PRACTICE #24: Don't resist change when you see God bringing something new into your life.

The LORD says, "I will guide you along the best pathway
for your life.
I will advise you and watch over you."
—PSALM 32:8

TONY

Things change. Sometimes abruptly and unexpectedly.

I discovered this as my football playing career was coming to an end. I had played in high school and college, and then began my career with the Pittsburgh Steelers, where I was a member of the 1979 Super Bowl–winning team. But by 1980, I had been traded twice, first to the San Francisco 49ers, and next to the New York Giants, within a twelve-month period. Then Ray Perkins, head coach of the Giants at the time, informed me near the end of training camp that he was cutting me from the team.

I was twenty-five years old and had been playing football for fourteen of those years. I loved the game, but as much as I wanted to continue playing, I could see the door closing on my career. It was disappointing. Rather than getting too discouraged or trying to eke out a little more playing time, I decided to pray about what God wanted to do with my life. As I did, I remembered an off-hand comment Coach Perkins made as he was releasing me: "Tony, you're very smart and have such a good approach to the game that I think you'd make a very good coach someday."

Soon I was back in Pittsburgh, working on Chuck Noll's staff for the Steelers, just two years after Coach Noll had traded me away. Not long after that, I met Lauren. I discovered that often when God moves us, He has great blessings in store if we simply follow His leading.

We need to remember that God never closes a door without opening another—or at least a window. Or sometimes even a vent! He always wants the best for us, so a door closing may lead to a period of rest, quiet, or waiting. In my case, I sat out the entire 1980 NFL season.

Just think, if my playing career hadn't ended when it did, I never would have met my wife. God had to change my life in order to *really* change my life! Here's the truth: We can't see the whole picture but God can.

That reminds me of a story I heard about two small boys who wanted to see a parade that was passing by. However, they were standing behind a wooden fence and the floats and marching bands were moving along on the other side. Suddenly one of the boys saw a knothole in the fence. Now they were able to watch the parade, within limits—the problem was that they couldn't see what had gone before, and they couldn't see what was coming.

That's a little like our lives. We can't see the full picture. But God can see it, and He never leaves us alone. He sees and controls our tomorrow.

Adventure Application: If your life were a parade, what would you say is in your line of sight right now? Would you compare it to a stunning float, a group of scary-looking clowns, or an out-of-sync marching band? What would you like to see next in the procession? Thank God for where He has placed you now, knowing He can see what comes next.

day 28

PRINCIPLE 2
STAY IN SYNC SPIRITUALLY.

UNCOMMON WISDOM

Your eternal word, O LORD,
stands firm in heaven.
Your faithfulness extends to every generation,
as enduring as the earth you created.

—PSALM 119:89-90

UNCOMMON PRACTICE

Take a few moments to select one of this week's practices to explore further. The related Adventure Application appears just below each practice. If you'd prefer to come up with a different way of living out that practice this week, feel free to discuss what that might look like.

- *Consider the input and wisdom of others when making decisions.*
  What decision do you or your family need to make? Review Jerry Clower's four questions for decision making, and then discuss how you might answer them in light of the options you are considering.

- *Plug into a church that offers solid biblical teaching and where you feel at home.*
  Is your church meeting your family's needs at this stage? If so, that's great. If not, what should you do?

- *Seek out an older couple who can model a strong marriage and family life.*
  Do you know a godly older couple to whom you can look for mentoring, wisdom, and guidance? Be sure to spend time with them. If you don't have such a couple in your life, try to identify one who could serve in that role. Take the first step to get to know them better this week.

- *Be open to the possibility that the Lord is speaking to you through the input of your spouse.*
  How can you do a better job of tuning in to your spouse and really listening to what he or she has to say? Remember that God may be sharing something He wants you to hear through him or her.

- *Share with each other the lessons you learn as you study the Bible.*
  Look to share at least one thing with your spouse each day this week that you learn in your private Scripture reading, devotional reading, or in a Bible study elsewhere. Encourage your spouse to add his or her insights to the discussion. You both will be doubly blessed.

- *Don't resist change when you see God bringing something new into your life.*
  If your life were a parade, what would you say is in your line of sight right now? Would you compare it to a stunning float, a group of scary-looking clowns, or an out-of-sync marching band? What would you like to see next in the procession? Thank God for where He has placed you now, knowing He can see what comes next.

UNCOMMON PRAYER

Take a few minutes to discuss any praises and needs you'd like to bring to God as a couple. Then, in addition to praying about those things together, use one or more of the following prayer prompts to ask God to help you stay in sync spiritually.

Praise God for the older family members, mentors, and pastors He's brought into your lives and the insights you've gained as they've shared their wisdom and experience.

Confess your need for God to give you the desire to spend regular time in His Word.

Ask the Holy Spirit to be at work in your mind and heart this week as you read the Bible, listen to messages and teaching, and talk with each other about what you're learning from your study of the Scriptures.

day 29
MISMATCHED PRIORITY

CORE PRACTICE #25:
Recognize that differing expectations are inevitable given
different upbringings.

....

You will decide on a matter, and it will be established for you, and
light will shine on your ways. —JOB 22:28, ESV

TONY

Growing up in a small town, Jackson, Michigan, my childhood
was filled with sports. Baseball, basketball, football—I wanted
to try pretty much anything that involved a ball and a score.
While I played on organized league teams, I was always ready
to join any game that might break out in the neighborhood
or at school. Many nights in high school I would ride with
friends to Lansing, Ann Arbor, Romulus—anywhere within
driving distance, and we'd play basketball under the lights into
the evening.

Finally, after high school I cut my serious pursuit of sports
down to two: football and basketball. I played both as a fresh-
man at the University of Minnesota. When I wasn't in class, my
time was spent doing homework, being at practice, and working out on my own. After graduating, I was blessed to be able
to play professional football.

By the time we met, Lauren's experiences during high school
and college couldn't have been more different. As a teenager, she
spent most of her time outside of class working. In the summers, when I would have been playing three or four sports and
barely coming home to eat, she shared a paper route with her

brothers and worked at local restaurants and department stores in Pittsburgh. That continued after high school graduation. While I was playing sports at Minnesota, she was at Duquesne University, literally working her way through college.

My parents wanted me to work hard, to be sure. However, they encouraged me to follow my passion in athletics, believing I could learn many important life lessons through those sports. Lauren's parents, on the other hand, had an entrepreneurial bent, and they believed their children would learn life lessons and skills most effectively through employment.

Of course, Lauren and I didn't realize how intrinsic those differences were when we were standing at the altar on our wedding day. We didn't really understand that we were bringing entirely different life experiences, family and sibling dynamics, and expectations into the marriage. Yet such differences are inevitable when two families are merging into one.

One reason that Lauren and I advocate premarital counseling so strongly is that it can help couples understand the need to recognize and resolve issues like this one. Sometimes just being aware of the different perspectives two people bring into marriage is all that's really needed.

When we got married, Lauren and I didn't magically have all the answers about whether our children should work, play sports, or do both. In fact, we didn't even realize that sports vs. work was a question until much later when our children were older. Lauren thought the answers were obvious.

So did I.

Deciding what activities to encourage our kids to pursue turned out to be yet another situation where communication between us was critical. We'd already established routines that allowed us to talk regularly, so we were able to talk through these issues. Communicating helped us understand each other's point of view, and we reached a place of compromise so we could help our children pursue their passions while learning life's lessons in a way that made sense to both of us.

Adventure Application: Take a few minutes to discuss what activities or values were emphasized in your home growing up. Has that resulted in any expectations for your own family? If so, does that concern either of you?

day 30
FAMILY PORTRAIT

CORE PRACTICE #26:
Be open to exploring new or different family traditions.

....

So Moses and Aaron were brought back to Pharaoh. "All right," he told them, "go and worship the LORD your God. But who exactly will be going with you?"

Moses replied, "We will all go—young and old, our sons and daughters, and our flocks and herds. We must all join together in celebrating a festival to the LORD." —EXODUS 10:8-9

TONY

We all grow up with certain family traditions. Many center around the holidays—specifically, holiday meals. Often even the kids know which aunt or cousin can be counted on to bring the sweet potato casserole or chocolate chip cheesecake. Then come the games—definitely football at Thanksgiving and maybe Monopoly or some other board game at Christmas.

No matter how we grew up—even if it wasn't in the best of family environments—we all cling to certain traditions when we start our own families. These customs help us remember who we are and who we should be. They connect us to our roots and remind us of where we came from.

Lauren and I treasure the traditions we brought into our marriage, and we incorporated a number of them into our own family life. But we have also started some new ones, and I have to give Lauren the credit for that. One of our favorites requires the cooperation of our entire family at Christmastime.

Lauren loves Christmas for a number of reasons, the most

important being that we remember and celebrate the birth of our Savior, Jesus Christ. But she also likes it because it started what has become an annual event for us—the Dungy family picture. When I was growing up, we never gathered for a family picture, but I was open to the idea when Lauren first brought it up. And now, it definitely qualifies as a tradition! Every year we send out a Christmas card to family and friends that is designed around a creatively arranged photograph of our entire family. And, of course, everyone has to wear matching attire.

At first it was pretty easy to arrange—Lauren simply had to coordinate the two of us. Then it became the two of us with Tiara, and then with Jamie. But as our family has grown to nine children and as our older kids have moved to different parts of the country, getting everyone together has been a little harder. (Also finding an outfit for twenty-something Tiara that will match what baby Jaden will wear can be really difficult.)

But somehow, Lauren always manages to pull it off. And our entire family has come to expect that we will have that holiday picture taken—all of us smiling and looking at the camera the moment the baby is not crying. In fact, we see it as just another one of the many miracles of Christmas! Our friends tell us they look forward to getting the Dungy Christmas card each year, and I personally hear a lot of compliments on how great the photo is—even with me in the picture.

Adventure Application: What Christmas traditions do you and your family particularly enjoy? If nothing comes to mind, poll your family and come up with something you could do together as an enjoyable way to celebrate the meaning of Christmas. Family Life has compiled a list that might spark some ideas. See http://www.familylife.com/articles/topics/holidays/featured /christmas/10-great-ideas-for-christmas-traditions.

day 31
WHEN THE FISH ARE BITING

CORE PRACTICE #27:
Don't expect your spouse to be able to read your mind.

....

*Don't look out only for your own interests, but take an interest
in others, too.* —PHILIPPIANS 2:4

TONY

One of the hardest adjustments I had to make after I got married was learning to communicate my plans to Lauren. When I was single, I had gotten into a routine I was used to, but I'd never had to share my schedule with anyone else or worry that they were even thinking about it. If I had a change in plans, it was no big deal. It didn't impact anyone but me.

As a newly married man, it never occurred to me that Lauren had no idea what I was thinking. *I* knew what I was doing after work, and I simply assumed that everyone, including Lauren, knew I was fine.

What was I doing?

Fishing, of course.

In my single days, I often used my free time from the Steelers to head out for a quick fishing trip on a nearby river or lake. Once we married, I quickly learned to give Lauren my projected schedule. But if I told her I thought I'd be home by six and the fish were really biting, I might decide to stay a little longer and . . . well, I never thought to find a phone to call Lauren. Certainly she would know I couldn't leave if the fish were biting!

Lesson number one: Don't assume, communicate!

Without a call from me, there was no way for Lauren to

know that I was safe or when I would be home. Her concern led her to imagine a more serious scenario than biting fish to explain why I was so late.

We tend to think inwardly, and our focus tends to be on ourselves. We don't mean it in a malicious or arrogant way, but it is rather a condition of our selfish, sinful human nature. The apostle Paul says there is a better way. Just after directing the Philippians not to "look out only for your own interests, but take an interest in others," he urged them to adopt the same attitude as Christ, who gave up His "divine privileges" and "humbled himself in obedience to God and died a criminal's death on a cross" (vv. 7-8). Following Jesus' example is not easy, and I often find myself turning to God to ask for His help.

I mean well, but my tendency is to view the world and my marriage through my own lens. Lauren and I have now been married for more than thirty years, but she still cannot read my mind or know my precise location if I don't communicate. Because her feelings and needs matter to me, I don't want to catch her off guard. In fact, I've found it is much more productive to remind her of my plans for the day, even if she simply shrugs and says, "I knew that."

Nowadays I'm really grateful for cell phones since the fish still tend to bite at unpredictable times!

Adventure Application: Discuss whether you or your spouse can think of any recurring issues that come up because one of you thinks that the other should simply "know that by now." Take a step back. How might you address that concern? It's better to err on the side of clarity and communication than to remain stuck in uncertainty or resentment.

day 32
TWO-PART HARMONY

CORE PRACTICE #28:
Learn to adjust to and accept the "quirks" of your spouse's side of the family.

....

May God, who gives this patience and encouragement, help you live in complete harmony with each other, as is fitting for followers of Christ Jesus. Then all of you can join together with one voice, giving praise and glory to God, the Father of our Lord Jesus Christ. Therefore, accept each other just as Christ has accepted you so that God will be given glory. —ROMANS 15:5-7

Lauren

"It's not the things I don't understand about the Bible that bother me," says pastor and author Bill Hybels, "it's the things I understand with perfect clarity and don't comply with that keep me up at night."

Who doesn't long to live in "complete harmony" with others so that we can praise and glorify God, as Paul instructs above? Yet when we get to verse 7, we see why peaceful living can sometimes feel so elusive. One of the secrets, we read, is that we must "accept each other just *as Christ has accepted you*" (emphasis added). With absolute love? Unconditional forgiveness? A desire for the other person's best? Is that even possible?

Marriage—the union of two very different people—sure puts that to the test. That can be particularly true when the couple's extended families are involved. After all, every family has its share of interesting idiosyncrasies, which both husband and wife must adjust to.

As we mentioned earlier, Tony's and my families are very different. We love them both, but we learned early on that to love our in-laws as Christ loved them, we needed His help as we adjusted to their ways and they began to adjust to ours.

I had grown up in a family that generally followed a pretty structured schedule. Tony's parents, on the other hand, were a bit less concerned with planning. Or, if they followed a structure, I couldn't figure it out. They lived in Michigan for all of their married life, but they loved to come and visit us from the time Tony was coaching with the Pittsburgh Steelers.

Tony's mom and dad were a joy to have in our home, but whenever they planned a visit, they never told us what time to expect them. I always wanted to be sure to have a meal ready for them when they pulled up, but not knowing when they would arrive often made that difficult.

To avoid resentment from blocking the harmony between us, I eventually realized I needed to speak up about this. Tony encouraged me to do so as well. I finally did, describing the pressure I felt as I tried to be ready for their visit without knowing when they were going to arrive. I explained that sometimes Tony, the children, and I worried about whether something happened to them on the road. And, of course, I wanted to find out whether they planned to eat on the way or whether I should have a meal waiting for them.

Talking to them helped. They hadn't realized we were concerned. Not only that, but Tony's mom explained that they often left just as soon as her husband came home from work—but she didn't always know when that would be. In the days before cell phones, they didn't always take the time to call once they got on the road. After our conversation, they did a much better job of letting us know when to expect them. At the same time, I learned not to get quite so caught up in trying to schedule every detail of their visit.

I wasn't the only one who had to learn to adjust to my in-laws' differences. Tony had to get used to my twin brother, Loren, freely offering his advice. When we were building our home in Tampa, Loren wanted to make sure we were getting our money's worth, so he appointed himself as an absentee project manager. When he was in town, he would make regular visits on-site to check on the construction. He would shake windows and peel back insulation to see what it was covering and to make sure it was the correct R rating. He was quick to give his opinion—occasionally to us, but usually to the builder—as to the workmanship.

But Loren's heart was good, and Tony learned to appreciate having another set of eyes on our home's progress. Tony and I even got a good laugh when we realized that my brother's visits usually coincided with a home football game.

Adventure Application: Have you noticed some interesting habits or behaviors on your spouse's side of the family? Make a point this week to appreciate those family members better and accept or adjust to the way they are.

day 33
NOT WRONG, JUST DIFFERENT

CORE PRACTICE #29:
Train yourself to look for your spouse's strengths in his or her differences.

....

In his grace, God has given us different gifts for doing certain things well. So if God has given you the ability to prophesy, speak out with as much faith as God has given you. If your gift is serving others, serve them well. If you are a teacher, teach well. —ROMANS 12:6-7

TONY

Why is it that when we learn that we have more differences from our spouses than we realized, we tend to be a bit bothered—maybe even wonder if something is wrong? Perhaps you and your spouse would feel better if you were a little more alike, had all the same interests, and enjoyed similar activities. But as the Scripture above points out, that's not how God made us.

We have each been created with unique gifts, abilities, and talents, unlike anyone else. God reminded us why He created each of us differently when He spoke to Jeremiah about His purpose for him: "I knew you before I formed you in your mother's womb. Before you were born I set you apart and appointed you as my prophet to the nations" (Jeremiah 1:5).

Just as God created Jeremiah with a unique assignment in mind, so He has a different—if complementary—purpose for you and your spouse. When bothered by any of the differences we discover in each other, we can feel a sense of calm and peace, knowing that God designed us that way. Different is not bad. It's good. It's great.

It's just . . . different.

The key is to see your differences, not as negatives or weaknesses, but as simply a part of who each of you are. A part that was placed there by the God who created you.

One definite difference between Lauren and me that we've come to appreciate over the years is our reaction to challenges. Lauren's tendency is to respond much more quickly and energetically to situations than I do. I tend to be more laid-back, listen more, and be more reflective as I take in all I see and hear. But as different as we are, both personalities work well for our marriage. This has never been more evident than in helping our son Jordan with his medical issues.

At times, Lauren's more emotional nature has enabled us to get things done faster for him. Because of her initiative, we've sometimes gotten a second opinion or tried a different procedure that has made a positive difference. But there are times—often the same times—when my calmer approach has helped us both process the information before us in a way that works out best for Jordan's medical health. Neither Lauren's nor my approach is the right way. Neither is the wrong way. They are simply different. After the dozen-plus surgeries that our precious son has gone through, Lauren and I can say with confidence that Jordan has been well served by having a mom and a dad who respond in completely different ways but always with his best interest in mind.

Adventure Application: Take turns mentioning one characteristic of your spouse that makes you completely different—but that you've come to appreciate during your marriage. Can you name a situation when you realized just how much you valued your spouse for that reason?

day 34
WHO DOES WHAT?

CORE PRACTICE # 30:
Allow each spouse to take the lead in the area of his or her strength.

God has given each of you a gift from his great variety of spiritual gifts.
Use them well to serve one another. Do you have the gift of speaking?
Then speak as though God himself were speaking through you. Do you
have the gift of helping others? Do it with all the strength and energy
that God supplies. Then everything you do will bring glory to God
through Jesus Christ. —1 PETER 4:10-11

Lauren

The first home that Tony and I purchased together was located
on two acres. One chore that I actually looked forward to was
mowing the lawn. Growing up, my brothers always got to work
outside while all of my sister's and my chores seemed to be
inside. Now I would get to be the one enjoying the smell of
freshly cut grass and an hour in the sun.

Given the size of our lot and our full-time jobs, I convinced
Tony that we should buy a riding mower at Sears. As we stood
before the display of mowers, I noticed the salesman directing
all of his comments toward Tony. I wanted to shout at him, "No,
no; look at me! I need the information! I'm the one who's going
to be riding the lawn mower!" Thankfully, Tony finally pointed
at me and told the man, "She's got a few more questions."

I'm glad Tony wasn't threatened by that, just as I never
minded when the kids asked Tony if he could make them pancakes on Saturday mornings. Mowing the lawn and making
breakfast are just two of a host of responsibilities that every

family has as it grows. The question often becomes just *who* is in charge of each of the various areas of responsibility? Should it be the person best equipped for the task? Or should we follow cultural expectations as to who does what?

Some look to Paul's instructions to the believers at Ephesus to help answer these questions: "For wives, this means submit to your husbands as to the Lord. For a husband is the head of his wife as Christ is the head of the church. He is the Savior of his body, the church" (Ephesians 5:22-23).

The problem comes when this passage is taken out of context and interpreted contrary to God's true intent. God has gifted us all differently; so, as a married couple, why not use those gifts to the benefit of your marriage?

Tony is a tremendous football coach, and in particular, he is an exemplary head coach. And that's not just my opinion, even though I'm his most biased fan. One reason for his success as a head football coach is his ability to identify the gifts and talents of his assistant coaches and staff. Once he does that, as he discussed in *The Mentor Leader*, he equips, enables, and empowers each of them to lead by using the skill sets they have been given for the good of the players, other coaches, and ultimately the team.

No successful football coach would put his best six-foot-five-inch, 330-pound offensive lineman in as a wide receiver and expect to have an effective passing game. Nor would he play his top defensive end at quarterback. No good head coach would have the offensive coordinator prepare the game plan all week, run practices before the next game, and then on game day call all the plays himself.

A marriage is really no different, at least if it is to function at a high level. Why assume a husband or wife should take responsibility for an area he or she is not wired for? Why not allow each partner to contribute to the marriage and the family by using his or her God-given strengths for its benefit?

That's why Tony is such a great husband, father, and leader within our family. But just because he's gifted in leading doesn't mean he has to be the one doing or deciding everything. Years ago, he and I assessed where our different areas of giftedness are. For instance, he is good at managing finances and loves to do that, so he does. I am skilled at organizing and scheduling, and I have a gift for hospitality—so I take the lead in those areas.

Together we merge our strengths and gifts for the good of the team—our marriage and family. Especially when it means I'm on the riding lawn mower while Tony is inside flipping pancakes.

Adventure Application: This week, talk with your spouse about areas of responsibility you each have within your family. Are there some household chores that one spouse would be better at and enjoy more, regardless of what society says is the "proper" role?

day 35

PRINCIPLE 3

MANAGE EXPECTATIONS AND APPRECIATE YOUR DIFFERENCES.

UNCOMMON WISDOM

Continue to show deep love for each other, for love covers a multitude of sins. —1 PETER 4:8

UNCOMMON PRACTICE

Take a few moments to select one of this week's practices to explore further. The related Adventure Application appears just below each practice. If you'd prefer to come up with a different way of living out that practice this week, feel free to discuss what that might look like.

- *Recognize that differing expectations are inevitable given different upbringings.*
  Take a few minutes to discuss what activities or values were emphasized in your home growing up. Has that resulted in any expectations for your own family? If so, does that concern either of you?

- *Be open to exploring new or different family traditions.*
  What Christmas traditions do you and your family particularly enjoy? If nothing comes to mind, poll your family and come up with something you could do together as an enjoyable way to celebrate the meaning of Christmas. Family Life has compiled a list that might spark some ideas.

See http://www.familylife.com/articles/topics/holidays
/featured/christmas/10-great-ideas-for-christmas-traditions.

- *Don't expect your spouse to be able to read your mind.*
  Discuss whether you or your spouse can think of any
  recurring issues that come up because one of you thinks
  that the other should simply "know that by now." Take
  a step back. How might you address that concern? It's
  better to err on the side of clarity and communication
  than to remain stuck in uncertainty or resentment.

- *Learn to adjust to and accept the "quirks" of your spouse's
  side of the family.*
  Have you noticed some interesting habits or behaviors
  on your spouse's side of the family? Make a point this
  week to appreciate those family members better and
  accept or adjust to the way they are.

- *Train yourself to look for your spouse's strengths in his or
  her differences.*
  Take turns mentioning one characteristic of your spouse
  that makes you completely different—but that you've
  come to appreciate during your marriage. Can you name
  a situation when you realized just how much you valued
  your spouse for that reason?

- *Allow each spouse to take the lead in the area of his or
  her strength.*
  This week, talk with your spouse about areas of
  responsibility you each have within your family. Are
  there some household chores that one spouse would be
  better at and enjoy more, regardless of what society says
  is the "proper" role?

UNCOMMON PRAYER

Take a few minutes to discuss any praises and needs you'd like to bring to God as a couple. Then, in addition to praying about those things together, use one or more of the following prayer prompts to ask God to help you learn to manage your expectations and appreciate your differences.

Praise the Father for specific differences He built into each of you, as well as into your children and other family members.

Confess any friction in your marriage because of your impatience or frustration over some of your differences and unmet expectations.

Ask the Holy Spirit to equip you with the patience, discernment, and kindness you need to encourage your spouse in the areas of his or her giftedness, as well as to accept his or her different approaches to some areas of life.

day 36
HELP WANTED

CORE PRACTICE #31:
Seek outside counsel when expectations and differences are too great to work through on your own.

....

Without wise leadership, a nation falls; there is safety in having many advisers. —PROVERBS 11:14

TONY

The *New York Times* called him "the country's least likely love guru" and said he sounds like Gomer Pyle.[5] And yet couples flock to his conferences and buy his books. In fact, one that he wrote in 1992, *The 5 Love Languages*, often ranks as the best-selling book on marriage. His name? Gary Chapman.

Long before he was recognized as a marriage expert, however, couples in crisis were drawn to this down-to-earth pastor. Early in his career, he began teaching classes on marriage and family at his church. Once people noticed that he was a good, empathetic listener, many dropped by his office to talk. Over the years, he began to notice that spouses often struggled because they didn't feel loved. "If you feel loved by your spouse, the whole world is right," he said. "If the love tank is empty, the whole world can begin to look dark."[6]

Interestingly, Chapman admits that the early years of his own marriage were so difficult that if he hadn't made a vow to God, he would have left his wife. Over time, they learned to accept and accommodate their differing needs and today have a thriving marriage.

Chapman's popularity—both in his local church when he

was a young pastor and in the wider culture today—point to the hunger many couples have to unlock the key to a stronger marriage. He proves that sometimes we have to look outside ourselves for the wisdom and biblical perspective we need.

In fact, that's one reason why Lauren and I are such big proponents of premarital counseling. The pastor who married us met with us beforehand to talk about a number of issues, many of which weren't first and foremost on our minds, but which turned out to be very helpful and practical as we began our marriage. We covered a lot of ground—from the biblical view of marriage to conflict resolution to budgeting—and because of this counseling, we avoided some inappropriate reactions and wrong decisions.

Yet even with the best premarital counseling, marriage is not always a smooth and level journey. In addition to wonderful moments of joy, life is sprinkled with disappointing lows, painful heartaches, and moments of despair. At these times, we're often most tempted to pull away from each other. While we all need time to think and be by ourselves, if we become disconnected, it's important to seek guidance and help from someone else.

If that's where you find yourselves today, reach out to a friend or a pastor, or find a professionally trained Christian counselor who specializes in working with married couples. Don't let what others may think stop you—God has placed people around you with the ability to help you and your spouse strengthen your marriage commitment and guide you through the valleys.

Don't settle for the wisdom of a so-called marriage expert on the newest talk show or reality TV program. Don't even rush out to buy the book by the latest relationship guru—unless his or her advice is grounded in the bestselling book of all time, the Bible.

Adventure Application: As you consider your marriage today, are you feeling hopeful or helpless? If you need godly guidance, talk about whom you might turn to for direction or help.

day 37
PICKING YOUR BATTLES

CORE PRACTICE #32:
Be wise when picking your battles, understanding that your spouse probably doesn't intend his or her weaknesses to cause you grief.

···

Anyone who listens to my teaching and follows it is wise, like a person who builds a house on solid rock. Though the rain comes in torrents and the floodwaters rise and the winds beat against that house, it won't collapse because it is built on bedrock. But anyone who hears my teaching and doesn't obey it is foolish, like a person who builds a house on sand. When the rains and floods come and the winds beat against that house, it will collapse with a mighty crash. —MATTHEW 7:24-27

Lauren

Our hometown, Tampa, and nearby areas have been in the headlines recently because of sinkholes that have unexpectedly swallowed sections of streets and homes. Though geologists point out that sinkholes are natural and usually develop over hundreds of years, when they develop rapidly, they can be deadly. That's exactly what happened in early 2013. Jeff Bush, who was in his bed, sank thirty feet when a sinkhole opened under his room. Tragically, he was never found.

So you might understand why I was concerned when I saw some substantial cracking at the back of our house. When our next-door neighbors told Tony and me that they had a sinkhole, we became even more uneasy—or perhaps I should say that I became more uneasy.

If you've ever watched Tony on the sidelines during a football game, then you might not be surprised to hear that he remained laid-back and relaxed about the sinkhole news. His attitude was, *Well, let's just get it fixed. . . . Maybe I'll call a contractor next week, and then we can get a couple of estimates.*

On the other hand, I was thinking, *What? You don't mind that our kids' safety is at risk? Are you serious? Honey, we've got to get the house foundation stabilized—now!*

Guess who was on the phone the next day? To me, the possibility that a sinkhole could be developing under our house was deadly serious. Tony didn't feel the same sense of urgency; in fact, if it had been up to him, I suspect we might still be searching the Yellow Pages for a contractor.

Thankfully, most disagreements are not so serious. Tony and I may dispute a politician's recent comments or whether a particular actor or actress should have taken a certain role in a movie or whether we should take the kids to the pool or to the beach. In fact, such differences of opinion don't even rise to the level of a quarrel.

During the course of any given day, I've discovered that Tony and I disagree on matters that we can view simply as contrasting ways of doing things. The key for us is to recognize these moments for what they are—simply differences that don't matter in the bigger, more important aspects of our marriage.

I put "our sinkhole story" in another category. That threatened my family's safety, so I felt it needed to be confronted. I was not willing to accept Tony's low-key approach. Whether I refer to that example as a "battle" or not might be a matter of semantics. After all, Tony backed my decision to deal with the cracking foundation immediately, so it didn't become an issue between us.

Yet it did illustrate an important point: We need to learn the difference between conflict worth engaging in and minor disagreements that are best let go. It comes down to knowing the foundational values and priorities of our marriage and our family. When the fundamentals upon which God has built our marriage come under attack, we need to stand up and confront wherever the threat may be coming from—our spouse or elsewhere.

For example, the times when I consider it crucial for me to take a stand include any actions, decisions, or suggested courses of action that are contrary to God's Word. I will also fight if one member of the family is showing disrespect to another. I will not sit by when I think anyone in my family is in physical, emotional, psychological, or spiritual danger. You might add your own nonnegotiable points to the list.

And at other times? When we disagree with our spouse over issues that carry no threat—except maybe to our ego—sometimes it's best just to smile and let it go.

Adventure Application: Keep a careful eye this week on those moments when you and your spouse disagree. Are those issues foundational to your marriage or family? If so, deal with them. Otherwise, accept the fact that you have differences and smile— at least once the moment has passed.

day 38
MULTIPLE ATTRACTIONS

CORE PRACTICE #33:
Recognize that God often brings together different types of people to complement each other and bring balance to a family.

....

If the whole body were an eye, how would you hear? Or if your whole body were an ear, how would you smell anything?

But our bodies have many parts, and God has put each part just where he wants it. How strange a body would be if it had only one part! Yes, there are many parts, but only one body. —1 CORINTHIANS 12:17-20

Lauren

One of the great things about living in Tampa is that we've got plenty of fun things to do close to home. We can plan a day at one of the sunny beaches on the Gulf of Mexico or visit the terrific Lowry Park Zoo. We also can drive to Busch Gardens right here in Tampa or to Disney World and Universal Studios, which are a little over an hour away in Orlando. All these choices sometimes lead to indecision. Even when we can decide on a beach, an outing, or an amusement park, deciding what to do once we're there can be a challenge because of the different ages and personalities in our family.

Neither Tony nor I are thrill seekers, to be sure. We'd both be happy riding the bumper cars at Busch Gardens or Dumbo the Flying Elephant at Disney World and then calling it a day after relaxing on a bench with some ice cream.

Jade, however, is bored on anything traveling slower than eighty miles an hour. And while she's headed toward a certain coaster, Jordan is pulling us toward the superheroes section of whatever park we're in. In the meantime, the little kids are hunting down the cartoon characters. They like to watch them from a distance and maybe hesitantly head over toward them to have their picture taken.

Maybe.

This is, in so many ways, a microcosm of life. Our family is a collection of interests and opinions, just like the family of God. Individual members are created uniquely. Some like sports, and some like superheroes. Some enjoy thrill rides, and others prefer the bumper cars. Some are delighted to talk theology, while others look forward to going into prisons to help inmates develop new skills.

Our family, like the family of God, begins to function in a godly and productive way when Tony and I value each member's unique gifts and interests. What Tony applied to his football teams, I try to apply to our family: bringing out the best in each person while celebrating—not covering up—their differences. I want to encourage each child to make his or her own contribution for the good of our family while allowing him or her to grow individually as well.

And so Tony and I don't get to spend all our time on the bumper cars or eating ice cream. Rather we see the superheroes, figure out who will reluctantly accompany Jade on the roller coaster, and visit with the cartoon characters. In the midst of it all, we want to help our children realize that even if something isn't their favorite attraction, they need to create time for the activities that are important to others.

Much like we need to do as part of God's family.

Adventure Application: What are ways in which the individuals in your family are different? Are you making time to watch an action movie with your husband, if that's his thing? Is he making time to watch a romantic comedy—or your favorite—with you?

day 39
A FRESH PERSPECTIVE

CORE PRACTICE #34:
Expect that you will see things differently at times.

....

No, dear brothers and sisters, I have not achieved it, but I focus on this one thing: Forgetting the past and looking forward to what lies ahead, I press on to reach the end of the race and receive the heavenly prize for which God, through Christ Jesus, is calling us. Let all who are spiritually mature agree on these things. If you disagree on some point, I believe God will make it plain to you. But we must hold on to the progress we have already made. —PHILIPPIANS 3:13-16

TONY

If I ever took a Rorschach inkblot test, I probably wouldn't want the results published. I'm not even sure I would want Lauren or any of my children to know the results.

As I understand it, the Rorschach—named for its creator, Hermann Rorschach—is a psychological test consisting of ten inkblots printed on cards. Five of the cards are printed in black and white; the other five are printed in color. The test's supposed purpose is to help psychologists examine a person's personality characteristics and level of emotional functioning. It may even be used to determine if the patient has thought disorders. No matter what, I'm absolutely positive that I wouldn't want to know any of that information, let alone have it shared with others.

I don't even think I need to take tests like that; after all, I've discovered a lot about myself simply because I'm married. For instance, Lauren and I have learned that I'm the practical one.

I tend to point out why it might be prudent to wait or collect more information before making a decision. Lauren, on the other hand, is generally ready to move ahead on a decision if we have prayed about it and it could benefit our family. She points out that we can never know everything beforehand or know what will happen in the future.

A number of years ago, she suggested we buy an RV. She reminded me how much we love the outdoors and camping, and with all our kids—well, an RV seemed like a good way to travel. We had rented RVs several times and always had a lot of fun, but I pointed out the downsides of owning such a large vehicle. For about six years, my practical arguments worked— we simply didn't have a place to store anything that size. Then, a dealer out in Oregon told us if we bought one from him, we could park it on his lot. My saving grace was gone, and we're now the proud owners of an RV. The kids have loved it and, to my surprise, I have too.

Because of this experience and others like it, I know Lauren and I see things in the same general way, but we nearly always see things just a bit differently. We have distinct abilities and personalities that have been developed and refined through our life experiences. That means that, even though our values and priorities align, we often approach issues and decisions in slightly different ways.

Our contrasting viewpoints, we've learned, are not a bad thing. In fact, they can actually help us develop an even stronger bond if we recognize that each of us, with our differences and individual viewpoints, is a gift from God to the other.

Adventure Application: This week, be particularly sensitive to the times you and your spouse see things or react to things differently. Jot them down. In a quiet moment later, pray over this list and give thanks to God for those differences.

day 40
DON'T SIT ON THE SIDELINES

CORE PRACTICE #35:
Engage in activities you both enjoy together, but allow each other to maintain separate interests as well.

....

Love each other with genuine affection, and take delight in honoring each other. —ROMANS 12:10

Lauren

I have recently gotten into triathlons. Seriously into them. I love the different workouts and the way my body feels after training, whether I'm riding my bike, swimming laps, or running. I also like the training days when we transition between riding bikes and running.

Tony, however, does not like running. At all. He does love riding bikes, and we've been riding together for years. When I'm going to train on the bike, he's happy to tag along, but he doesn't enjoy swimming as much, and of course, running with me would definitely be demonstrating sacrificial love. I'm like that, too, in other ways. I enjoy participating in sports but not watching them. Therefore, going with Tony to watch a game is not my first choice of things to do.

However, we've learned to do things together that we don't share a common interest in, and to let the other enjoy the things he or she really loves. Tony recently ran a 5K race with me after training for a while. And, of course, I've watched plenty of football games with him. Triathlons? He'll probably sit those out, as I will his all-day fishing trips.

I've noticed, however, that some couples believe that if their interests aren't mutually compatible, then their marriage can't be successful. The reality is that God made each of us unique, with certain abilities and disabilities—as well as interests. Some of those passions turn out to be like those of our spouse, and we should certainly look to cultivate those.

But sometimes—in fact, often—they are different.

Neither our differences nor our similarities mean we are incompatible. No matter how different two people may be, compatibility depends in large measure on our desire to want the best for each other—especially within a marriage covenant.

Tony supports my triathlon training by watching the kids when I work out and by bringing the whole family to my races. It's always good to have his encouragement! And I don't resent his desire to watch sports—that's how he's wired. I read fiction, and lots of it. Tony thinks it's a waste of time and would rather read about history. He's fine with me going out to my book club, and I'm more than happy to let him read his nonfiction.

In the meantime, most every Tuesday during the school year we read to elementary school kids together through our Dungy Family Foundation. Children's books—a genre we can agree upon!

Though we look to share in activities we both enjoy whenever possible, rather than trying to force our interests on each other all the time, we recognize that compatibility is enhanced through our respect and support of each other's differences. I'll try things that are important to Tony, and he'll try things that are important to me. But if one of us doesn't really connect with the other's interest, we'll look for something else to do together . . . like read picture books to third graders!

Adventure Application: What is something that you and your spouse can do together? Does one of you have an interest that has fallen by the wayside because the other isn't interested? How could you better support each other?

day 41
HITTING THE HIGH NOTES

CORE PRACTICE #36:
Model appreciation of differences by treating each of your children as an individual with distinct needs at school and interests at home.

....

As the boys grew up, Esau became a skillful hunter. He was an outdoors-man, but Jacob had a quiet temperament, preferring to stay at home. Isaac loved Esau because he enjoyed eating the wild game Esau brought home, but Rebekah loved Jacob. —GENESIS 25:27-28

TONY

Lauren and I want to introduce our children to music, per-haps to see who will become a musician of some note (pun intended). To help make that happen, we have a piano in our living room. Lauren has played the piano since childhood and still does today, and our initial dream was to have all of our kids become pianists. Okay, maybe not concert pianists—we would have loved to see any of them take that path if it turned out to be an area of giftedness, but we at least hoped they'd become proficient in playing piano and appreciate the joys of playing a musical instrument.

And so at one time or another during their childhood years, all of our children took piano lessons. We discovered that they didn't all have the same skill or interest in playing the piano or *any* musical instrument. And as much as Lauren and I would have loved to have nine pianists in our family, we don't have any—at the moment.

Justin is the most musically inclined, and he has a great voice. But he followed Eric in gravitating toward football.

Jordan is all-consumed with electronics and gadgets, and he is the first one we go to whenever we have a computer question. Jade has been drawn to art and loves to do all varieties of artwork. All three children have developed a basic working knowledge of music through their piano lessons, but we have allowed them to explore their individual and unique interests. That is the way God made them—and that is what we want to try to help them develop.

This is true of the family of God as well. Lauren and I are involved in a number of worthwhile ministry outreaches. One that has been extremely gratifying to be involved with is Impact for Living. This ministry produces conferences, seminars, and a blog designed to help people uncover their unique passions and gifts. It then guides them to maximize those gifts as they better understand how God created them uniquely for this time in history.

Impact for Living emphasizes that our lives are comprised of four pillars of unique attributes that when maximized move us toward becoming all God created us to be. Those attributes are: purpose, passion, potential, and platform. In particular, the pillar of potential makes it clear that we each have been created by God with unique abilities and talents.

If you are a parent, you are purposefully positioned to nurture and help your own kids discover the unique ways God created them—even if that means putting up with clashing piano chords, paint spills, or cuts and bruises after the latest game.

Adventure Application: Maybe you've been trying to get your spouse or child to become someone God didn't create him or her to be. If so, consider a different approach, remembering that we are each wonderfully and uniquely created by God.

day 42

PRINCIPLE 3

MANAGE EXPECTATIONS AND APPRECIATE YOUR DIFFERENCES.

UNCOMMON WISDOM

Pride leads to conflict;
*   those who take advice are wise.*
Wealth from get-rich-quick schemes quickly disappears;
*   wealth from hard work grows over time.*
Hope deferred makes the heart sick,
*   but a dream fulfilled is a tree of life.*

PROVERBS 13:10-12

UNCOMMON PRACTICE

Take a few moments to select one of this week's practices to explore further. The related Adventure Application appears just below each practice. If you'd prefer to come up with a different way of living out that practice this week, feel free to discuss what that might look like.

- *Seek outside counsel when expectations and differences are too great to work through on your own.*
  As you consider your marriage today, are you feeling hopeful or helpless? If you need godly guidance, talk about whom you might turn to for direction or help.

- *Be wise when picking your battles, understanding that your spouse probably doesn't intend his or her weaknesses to cause you grief.*

Keep a careful eye this week on those moments when you and your spouse disagree. Are those issues foundational to your marriage or family? If so, deal with them. Otherwise, accept the fact that you have differences and smile—at least once the moment has passed.

- *Recognize that God often brings together different types of people to complement each other and bring balance to a family.*
  What are ways in which the individuals in your family are different? Are you making time to watch an action movie with your husband, if that's his thing? Is he making time to watch a romantic comedy—or your favorite—with you?

- *Expect that you will see things differently at times.*
  This week, be particularly sensitive to the times you and your spouse see things differently, or react to things differently. Jot them down. In a quiet moment later, pray over this list and give thanks to God for those differences.

- *Engage in activities you both enjoy together, but allow each other to maintain separate interests as well.*
  What is something that you and your spouse can do together? Does one of you have an interest that has fallen by the wayside because the other isn't interested? How could you better support each other?

- *Model appreciation of differences by treating each of your children as an individual with distinct needs at school and interests at home.*
  Maybe you've been trying to get your spouse or child to

become someone God didn't create him or her to be. If so, consider a different approach, remembering that we are each wonderfully and uniquely created by God.

UNCOMMON PRAYER

Take a few minutes to discuss any praises and needs you'd like to bring to God as a couple. Then, in addition to praying about those things together, use one or more of the following prayer prompts to ask God to help manage your expectations and appreciate your differences.

Praise the Father for activities that replenish or reinvigorate you, either as individuals or as a couple. Glorify Him for the different wonders in creation that make each of your hearts soar. Then spend a few minutes thanking the Lord for the differences you appreciate most about each other.

Confess any hurt or bitterness that has crept into your marriage because of unresolved differences of opinion. Ask the Lord to help you understand each other's hearts.

Ask God to bless your spouse in any particular work or endeavors he or she is involved in.

Petition the Lord to help you encourage your own children or those in your extended family as you see their gifts and interests develop.

day 43
ROLE REVERSAL

CORE PRACTICE #37:
Consciously think of your spouse as a valued teammate.

....

Now these are the gifts Christ gave to the church: the apostles, the prophets, the evangelists, and the pastors and teachers. Their responsibility is to equip God's people to do his work and build up the church, the body of Christ. —EPHESIANS 4:11-12

TONY

My work often takes me far from home. Whether I'm away for an NBC football broadcast or a speaking engagement, I usually don't give a lot of thought to how things are going at home. I know Lauren has everything under control.

It's only when Lauren goes away and I have to run things at home by myself that I appreciate all the details. It's the little things, which seem to be never ending, that trip me up. Getting all the kids dressed, fed, and off to school in the mornings; picking them up after school; making sure they finish their homework; getting them to practices or lessons; and then finally tucking them into bed for the night—as any parent knows, the to-do list never ends.

Every time I'm on my own with the kids at home, I'm reminded of how much Lauren has to do just to keep things running smoothly. And that doesn't include any time for herself! I think God uses these moments to reinforce to me not only how special Lauren is, but why raising a family is best done together, as teammates. Ironically, when I come home at the end of the day and ask Lauren about her day, she can't remember many specifics. However, because I've occasionally had to fill in for her, I've come to realize that all the details are time-consuming and critical.

Not only are our roles different, but mine have also been more public. If society were to assess the significance of my coaching or broadcasting roles compared to Lauren's, mine would probably be considered more important. However, in terms of value to society, that assessment couldn't be further from the truth.

God created each of us with specific roles and a specific purpose in mind. Though I realize that the apostle Paul is speaking specifically about spiritual gifts in today's Scripture, he is reminding the church in Ephesus that God gives each of us the ability to perform certain tasks. But we are each indispensable to the common goal of building up the church, whether we are working at a job site or at home.

How well I know it! Lauren will be traveling again soon, and while I love the time with the kids, they've made it clear that I'm nowhere near as competent as Mom when it comes to getting everything done.

Hurry home, sweetheart.

Adventure Application: You are teammates in a common cause, whether it is impacting the world, raising children, or completing some other task God has given you. Spend a few minutes discussing ways you might work together as a team.

day 44
ENJOYING GOD'S GOOD GIFTS—TOGETHER

CORE PRACTICE #38:
Make a special effort to learn more about your spouse's passions and interests.

....

It is a good thing to receive wealth from God and the good health to enjoy it. To enjoy your work and accept your lot in life—this is indeed a gift from God. —ECCLESIASTES 5:19

TONY

I've got to confess, I haven't always been so quick to notice the importance of some of the changes in Lauren's life. As a result, I haven't been as supportive initially as I should have been. I'm trying to be better at paying attention.

For example, in the last few years Lauren has gotten more engaged in physical fitness. She has always been in good shape, but she has become even more intentional about it. When she began running and discovered how much she enjoyed it, she ran more often and for much longer distances. She soon progressed to running in 5K races. Now she likes to enter half marathons. Her latest passion is triathlons—swim, bike, and run. To encourage Lauren as she trains, I decided I should join her. That way, not only would I be supporting her, but I would be honoring God myself by taking care of my body a little better. So I got involved in the running portion of her training programs.

I haven't gotten into the triathlon training as much though. The reason is simple—I like to swim for fun, but not to the point of total exhaustion. And I don't enjoy pushing myself so hard that I feel as if I'm drowning, even if I am only in four feet of water.

I decided that a better way for me to help was to research different training methods and the various watches and apps available to track the metrics of her workouts, such as her heart rate, distance, and split times. We've also looked into different boot camps and cross-training classes.

Not only has our partnership in the area of fitness made us both healthier, I've discovered just how interesting Lauren's new pursuits can be. She always seems to embrace activities that will help her become the person God wants her to be.

Lauren has also found that training for triathlons brings her great pleasure. And as Solomon points out in today's verses, God wants us to enjoy material blessings, including our health and our work. Of course, as anyone who has read Ecclesiastes knows, Solomon warns that if we idolize any of these blessings in themselves, we're likely to end up feeling as he did—that life is meaningless. The key, he says, is to "accept our lot in life," to keep "busy enjoying life" (Ecclesiastes 5:20), and to "remember your Creator" (12:6), the giver of all good gifts. That perspective, I've discovered, is much easier to maintain when Lauren and I live it out together.

After all, as I'm learning much about this new passion of hers, I'm learning much about her. Lauren and I even ran a 5K race together in May 2013 to benefit the Moffitt Cancer Center in Tampa. It was my first one, and for me, those 3.1 miles were not only a special effort, but also a true labor of love!

Adventure Application: In what ways are you and your spouse "busy enjoying life" together right now? If that's a tough question to answer, focus on an activity this week that one of you loves to do. Intentionally learn more about it or even engage in it together.

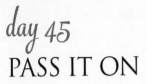

day 45
PASS IT ON

CORE PRACTICE #39:
Parent in a way that champions values, models character, and ensures each family member is doing what he or she needs to do that day.

But watch out! Be careful never to forget what you yourself have seen. Do not let these memories escape from your mind as long as you live! And be sure to pass them on to your children and grandchildren.

—DEUTERONOMY 4:9

Lauren

Since I am a former teacher and children's book author, it probably comes as no surprise that I have always encouraged our kids to embrace reading. One way I do that is by helping them see that reading can be fun. Some of our older children enjoy browsing for books on their e-readers or curling up with a sports magazine. If they're reading something worthwhile, I have no problem with that. I make trips to the library an adventure for our younger children by steering them toward books on topics I think would interest them. At home, I sometimes create a cozy spot for reading by placing comfy pillows and a stack of books in a corner or by draping blankets over a chair to create a tent.

I also make it a point to let my children see me enjoying good books; sometimes over dinner I even mention something I learned while reading a novel for my book club. The bottom line: I both champion reading and model it for my kids, even as I help them understand that learning and reading are important values in our family.

My approach to reading isn't all that different from the way

Tony and I have tried to pass along our commitment to biblical values. Our aim is not merely to get our children to obey us or a list of rules; we want them to experience the Lord's love for themselves by seeing how much joy and peace our relationship with God brings us. After all, our children are not our own. They are a sacred trust from the Lord to be cared for, nurtured, loved, and helped in every way possible to become all that God intends for them to be.

That same lesson is at the heart of today's Scripture passage, which comes from the book that some scholars refer to as Moses' farewell address to the Israelites. Moses knew that he was about to die and that Joshua would assume leadership of the people as they entered the Promised Land. As he urged the Israelites to follow God's rules and regulations, Moses stressed the importance of teaching their children to follow the Lord.

Moses' words are as timely for us today as they were back then. In the overall scheme of life and eternity, we have our children for such a brief time. Because of that, every moment of our lives should be about demonstrating and sharing with them the values they will need to live by. In everything we do for and with them, we need to model integrity, honesty, honor, and compassion, doing what is right in all settings and all ways. Will we do that perfectly? Of course not. But we can always testify to the greatness of God and what He's done for us. And we can always point them back to the book that contains all the wisdom they'll ever need—the Scriptures.

Adventure Application: Pick a character trait or godly value that you want your children to embrace and explain it to them. Spend some time during the next two weeks helping them see ways to live it out within the family and beyond.

day 46
OUTSIDE COUNSEL

CORE PRACTICE #40:
Seek coaching from trusted family members, friends, or counselors when you feel more like opponents than teammates.

Tune your ears to wisdom,
  and concentrate on understanding.
Cry out for insight,
  and ask for understanding.
Search for them as you would for silver;
  seek them like hidden treasures.

—PROVERBS 2:2-4

TONY

Many years ago, a frustrated woman arranged to meet with a psychologist. She spent the first meeting telling him how much she disliked her husband and that she intended to divorce him. "I want to hurt him all I can," she insisted.

"Well, then, I suggest you start showering him with compliments," the psychologist said, pointing out that her husband would come to view her as indispensable. "When he thinks you are completely devoted to him, start the divorce action. That is the way to really hurt him."

Months later the wife returned and told him she had followed the psychologist's suggestion.

"Good," said the psychologist. "Now's the time to file for divorce."

"Divorce?" the woman said indignantly. "Never. I love my husband dearly!"[7]

Marital struggles are no laughing matter, and yet there is some homespun wisdom in this humorous story. Sometimes we all need to find a wise, trustworthy counselor, family member, or friend to help us when we're locked in a misunderstanding we can't seem to get beyond. After all, the writer of Proverbs 2 urges us to "tune our ears," "cry out," "ask," "search," and "seek" when we need wisdom. If you and your spouse need pastoral or professional help, seek it out. If you simply need the input or different perspective of a close friend or family member, choose someone who is discerning and objective, whose advice has the best interest of your marriage at heart. But make sure you are seeking out the truth, and more specifically, God's truth. Be careful not to gravitate to someone who will simply commiserate with you and make things worse by taking your side at the expense of your marriage.

According to the book of Proverbs, the Lord promises the honest "a treasure of common sense" (2:7). So find a person of integrity who will help you seek God's wisdom, who will pray with you, and who will help you determine how to make your marriage all God intends it to be.

Adventure Application: If you need help resolving an issue, consider setting up a time this week to speak with a friend or counselor. Or you might choose to set aside time to pray for the Holy Spirit's wisdom in a matter. (Sunday's "Uncommon Prayer" section, found on page 120, might provide a good starting point.)

day 47
SHARED INVESTMENT

CORE PRACTICE #41:
Work to accomplish something important together; as you do, you'll see your marriage growing stronger.

....

I [Paul] have been a constant example of how you can help those in need by working hard. You should remember the words of the Lord Jesus: "It is more blessed to give than to receive." —ACTS 20:35

Lauren

When Tony was coaching the Buccaneers, we began participating in assemblies at Tampa schools with some of the players, but both my husband and I wanted to do something more personal and hands-on. That's when we began visiting classrooms and reading to the students. Since we started this venture before Tony retired, we couldn't commit to a regular schedule. If anything, we used his time away from the office to drop in on *our* children's schools.

But now we can visit two different elementary school classrooms in the Tampa area every Tuesday during the school year. We read one of our children's books out loud, talk about it with the students afterward, and donate books to encourage them to continue reading.

I taught elementary school for a number of years, so I know that one of the most gratifying moments in working with children is when you see the light go on in their eyes as they begin to connect with the words on the page. It is so rewarding to get a thank-you note from a teacher or a student letting us know that not only did he or she have fun, but we might have made a difference in a young person's life. Some of the children have even sent us books they've written!

Serving together has strengthened our marriage too. Tony received many accolades as an NFL coach, but my admiration for him has really grown as I've watched him interact with young boys who have no father figures at home. In addition, with six kids still living under our roof, we enjoy these few hours to ourselves every Tuesday. Our classroom visits often spark discussions later between us as Tony and I explore better ways to answer students' questions and make God's ideas clearer and more relevant to young people.

It's important to make memories—of any kind—with your spouse. Those often become some of the building blocks of your relationship. But the memories of the times you serve together are likely to be among the most enduring.

Adventure Application: What could you do together that would make a lasting impact? If you're drawing a blank, organizations like Big Brothers Big Sisters, The Salvation Army, or Habitat for Humanity might help you come up with ideas. If you already serve together, discuss how satisfied each of you is with that outreach.

day 48
IN THE SPOTLIGHT

CORE PRACTICE #42:
Be intentional about noticing and addressing the needs of your spouse and children.

....

Children, always obey your parents, for this pleases the Lord. Fathers, do not aggravate your children, or they will become discouraged.

—COLOSSIANS 3:20-21

TONY

Years ago a friend told me about a pivotal moment in his life. He was eating dinner with his wife and teenage son when he got up from the table to head to the kitchen stove to refill a bowl of broccoli. When he walked back into the dining room, he stopped.

There was a glow. Over his son's head.

He's now sure it wasn't really there. But at that moment, God seemed to put a spotlight on his son. In the midst of the trials with his teenager and daily life, it was as if the Lord was telling this father, "I've given you this family as a sacred trust. Raise your children, nurture them, build them up . . . but don't aggravate them. And for certain, don't take them for granted."

What a great point. We should recognize that our families are to be nurtured, built up, and helped to become all that God created them to be.

Our son Jordan was born with congenital insensitivity to pain, a rare and challenging condition. His nerve endings function and he can feel external stimuli, but any message involving pain or discomfort somehow doesn't make it to his brain.

Therefore, we have to help keep him from danger and examine him regularly for cuts, abrasions, or other injuries because he won't tell us about them—usually because he hasn't noticed them! Without proper attention, small wounds can develop into serious infections with complicated solutions.

Just as important as attending to Jordan's physical needs, however, has been dealing with his emotional and developmental ones. And those of our other children. Being present and perceptive is one of the best ways to avoid aggravating them.

With nine children, Lauren and I have to be especially careful not to overlook each other. I know it's possible to put off meeting our spouse's needs even when we're physically present. Instead of seeing our children with that angelic spotlight from the Lord, we settle into patterns of taking them for granted, figuring we'll spend time with them later. But when "later" comes, we're no longer plugged into their needs—or they are no longer willing to listen to us.

We need to be sensitive to our family's hurts and desires. Especially those that may not be spoken. Lauren and I have learned to communicate more effectively over the course of our marriage. With her help, I've learned to be perceptive to the things that are unspoken, to express my thoughts, and to listen when she starts to speak her mind. Or to follow up when she's slow to speak hers.

It isn't always easy, but keeping an eye on the needs of my family and asking for God's help to see them the way He does has paid great dividends.

Adventure Application: What is one specific way that you can address a need within your family—today?

day 49

PRINCIPLE 4

WORK AS A TEAM.

....

UNCOMMON WISDOM

Be of one mind, united in thought and purpose. —1 CORINTHIANS 1:10

UNCOMMON PRACTICE

Take a few moments to select one of this week's practices to explore further. The related Adventure Application appears just below each practice. If you'd prefer to come up with a different way of living out that practice this week, feel free to discuss what that might look like.

- *Consciously think of your spouse as a valued teammate.*
  You are teammates in a common cause, whether it is impacting the world, raising children, or completing some other task God has given you. Spend a few minutes discussing ways you might be able to work better together as a team.

- *Make a special effort to learn more about your spouse's passions and interests.*
  In what ways are you and your spouse "busy enjoying life" together right now? If that's a tough question to answer, focus on an activity this week that one of you loves to do. Intentionally learn more about it or even engage in it together.

- *Parent in a way that champions values, models character, and ensures each family member is doing what he or she needs to do that day.*
  Pick a character trait or godly value that you want your children to embrace and explain it to them. Spend some time during the next two weeks helping them see ways to live it out within the family and beyond.

- *Seek coaching from trusted family members, friends, or counselors when you feel more like opponents than teammates.*
  If you need help resolving an issue, consider setting up a time this week to speak with a friend or counselor. Or you might choose to set aside time to pray for the Holy Spirit's wisdom in a matter. (Sunday's "Uncommon Prayer" section, found on page 120, might provide a good starting point.)

- *Work to accomplish something important together; as you do, you'll see your marriage growing stronger.*
  What could you do together that would make a lasting impact? If you're drawing a blank, organizations like Big Brothers Big Sisters, The Salvation Army, Habitat for Humanity might help you come up with ideas. If you already serve together, discuss how satisfied each of you is with that outreach.

- *Be intentional about noticing and addressing the needs of your spouse and children.*
  What is one specific way that you can address a need within your family—today?

UNCOMMON PRAYER

Take a few minutes to discuss any praises and needs you'd like to bring to God as a couple. Then, in addition to praying about those things, use one or more of the following prayer prompts to ask for God's strength and wisdom as you seek to work as a team.

Praise God for the gift of each other and for uniting you in marriage so that together you are more than the sum of your individual parts.

Confess any areas where you might not be acting as teammates but as rivals or opponents.

Seek God's help in identifying a practical way in which you might serve your children, your extended family, or your community together.

Ask the Holy Spirit to give you wisdom on any issue within your marriage that seems to be pulling you apart.

day 50
ORDERING YOUR DAYS

CORE PRACTICE #43:
Establish household routines to cut down on confusion and stress,
but prioritize relationships over structure.

....

For God is not a God of disorder but of peace, as in all the meetings of
God's holy people. . . . But be sure that everything is done properly and
in order. —1 CORINTHIANS 14:33, 40

Lauren

I've always tried to keep an organized household, and with nine
children, organization is a necessity! From the beginning of the
school year in the fall, we establish routines for dinnertime,
homework periods, and bedtimes for each child, depending on
everyone's schedule and age. We've found those consistent routines not only help our children individually but also help our
household run more smoothly.

I learned a lot about running an orderly home from my
mother. I admired her ability to keep everything organized, and
I hope I'm passing on some of those same skills to our children.
For instance, whenever they come home, they know to put their
things in one of the cubbies in the laundry room. All the children have been assigned a different color on our master calendar
in the kitchen, so they can easily spot and prepare for their own
activities, practices, and school events.

Tony, on the other hand, is not as concerned about keeping things neat. That simply was not as high a priority in his
home growing up. So though his office is filled with amazing

pictures, mementos, and awards, it's also piled high with papers and boxes.

I suspect most couples are like us: one spouse is fairly orderly, while the other person doesn't even notice clutter. In our case, I've decided I need to pick my battles, and worrying about Tony keeping his study neat is not going to be one of them. On the other hand, Tony supports my efforts to keep an orderly home. He recognizes that everyone functions better when there's more structure and less confusion.

Tony and I both recognize that everything throughout creation has an orderliness to it. Order supports our purpose and our plans to implement whatever God has called us to do—whether as a spouse, a parent, a child, a coach, a teacher, or another professional. Order brings structure, making it easier to carry out our work and to run our homes.

But God prioritizes relationships—after all, Jesus went to the cross so our fellowship with Him could be restored. Likewise, Tony and I have learned to focus less on organization for its own sake and more on building strong relationships within our family. That's why, when we're expecting company, I've learned to simply shut the door to his study and why, when I come home from the store with another storage bin, Tony just smiles.

Adventure Application: How well do you and your spouse balance the need for both household order and relationship building? Which comes easier for you? What is one step you can take this week to strengthen the one that doesn't come as naturally?

day 51
COUPLE CARE

CORE PRACTICE #44:
Stay connected through date nights and joint activities.

....

In the same way, husbands ought to love their wives as they love their own bodies. For a man who loves his wife actually shows love for himself. —EPHESIANS 5:28

Lauren

Recently one of the couples in our Bible study, Yamilka and Dan Delgardo, celebrated their tenth wedding anniversary by holding a ceremony to renew their vows. Our entire group was invited to support them as they recommitted themselves to each other.

The celebration continued with a reception, complete with a meal and dancing. We had a great time. I actually got Tony out on the dance floor for a few dances! I suppose it was because so many of our friends were there and all the guys were dancing with their wives too. We hadn't danced together in a long time.

Afterward, several of the couples mentioned how enjoyable the evening had been, leading Tony to remark that we needed to do that more often. I quickly agreed!

We have had date nights throughout our marriage, but we realized we want to try doing a variety of activities during the evenings we've set aside to spend together. Amid all the demands at work and home, we want to do more things together simply for fun.

I don't know all the reasons couples drift apart, but I suspect one major cause is that they stop scheduling time together. In fact, I'm willing to guess that inattention creates more distance between couples than does a traumatic event or misbehavior by one spouse. Little by little, couples get so busy that mutual neglect slowly sets in. The bonds of commitment and caring begin to loosen.

Work naturally separates husbands and wives. Outside activities with friends of the same gender—sports teams, book clubs, civic clubs—may deepen the chasm. Even the demands of parenthood can turn our focus away from our spouse to our children. And busy as we are, all of us can find good excuses to skip date nights.

Yet as the apostle Paul points out in today's Scripture, we are to treat each other with the same care and respect we give our own bodies. Just as we take time to feed, clothe, and rest our bodies every day, so we should love our spouse—in part, by nurturing our relationship. That means we need to be intentional about creating opportunities to spend time together. Bible study, devotional, and prayer time together are essential. But so is doing things together just for fun, or simply to catch up with each other.

Regularly scheduled date nights are both a commitment and an opportunity to spend time with each other. We can dream together as we once did or look back and remember life's joys and challenges. We can simply enjoy each other as we do something fun together for a change—even if it is as simple as taking a walk in the park.

Whatever you do, one secret of an uncommon marriage is keeping those common interests . . . in common.

Adventure Application: Do you have a date night scheduled sometime in the next month? If not, take a few minutes to discuss a fun activity you could do together. Then get out your calendar and schedule it.

day 52
MAKING THE WAIT COUNT

CORE PRACTICE # 45: Don't rush into making major decisions.

....

I waited patiently for the LORD to help me,
and he turned to me and heard my cry.
He lifted me out of the pit of despair,
out of the mud and the mire.
He set my feet on solid ground
and steadied me as I walked along.
He has given me a new song to sing,
a hymn of praise to our God.

—PSALM 40:1-3

TONY

It was one of the most disappointing and heartbreaking moments of my life. I remember it all as if it were yesterday: clearing out my office at One Buccaneer Place late that night and then taking one final walk around the facility. That place had become my home away from home, and I wanted to spend a few minutes reflecting on all that was and all that might have been.

As I was leaving, I noticed the local Bay News 9 reporter recording footage of me—the former head coach of the Tampa Bay Buccaneers—loading boxes from my office into the back of my SUV. That footage would air repeatedly in the Tampa Bay area for the next few days.

I knew that being fired was an all-too-common reality in today's world, especially in the high-priced, high-stakes world of the National Football League. Acknowledging that made me feel a little better, as did believing that tomorrow would be easier, and the next day a little easier than that. After all, I still had my family, and we were all healthy. As I thought about it, I realized that God was simply closing a door and that He would open another one for me.

Still, I couldn't help but wonder what was next for me and my family. I wondered when I would hear from God. I hoped it would be soon. But Lauren and I also knew that we needed to give ourselves time to heal and reflect. We wanted to allow ourselves as much time as possible to pray and consider what other opportunities we might explore.

After we've experienced a job loss or other major life disruption, it's wise to wait patiently for God's comfort and direction. That doesn't happen by sitting back passively, but by praying, evaluating our situations, and reflecting on God's promises while leaning in to listen for His still, small voice. When we draw near to Him, He is able to direct us, to lift us out of the miry clay, and to put a new song in our mouths—as today's Scripture verses describe. Waiting is not always easy to do. Often after a major disappointment we want something to happen fast.

As badly as we wanted a quick answer as to the next step for our family, Lauren and I reminded ourselves to be patient as we prayed. We talked about trying to be sure we were following God's plans, not our own desires. The waiting ended for me and Lauren when the owner of the Indianapolis Colts left a lengthy message on our answering machine. Eventually it became clear that Jim Irsay's job offer was the answer we'd been looking for. It didn't come immediately—but it did teach us a little more about what waiting on God really means.

Adventure Application: Is your family facing a difficult decision? If so, are you waiting on God and listening for His voice? If you're not in decision-making mode now, how can you prepare yourself so you're ready the next time you face a major turning point?

day 53
LOVING WELL

CORE PRACTICE #46:
Consistently demonstrate support for your spouse.

....

Love is patient and kind. Love is not jealous or boastful or proud or
rude. It does not demand its own way. It is not irritable, and it keeps
no record of being wronged. It does not rejoice about injustice but
rejoices whenever the truth wins out. Love never gives up, never loses
faith, is always hopeful, and endures through every circumstance.

—1 CORINTHIANS 13:4-7

Lauren

"Why don't you call them and apply for the job? Take the initiative and show that you are interested and well-qualified for the
coaching position."

That's what I would say to Tony when he was an assistant
coach in the NFL and was wondering why he hadn't been contacted about a head-coaching position that had opened up. I
could sense his frustration at not getting any interviews, or even
phone calls from teams to gauge his interest and determine
whether he might be a good candidate.

Tony reminded me that every team knew that he was out
there. What he needed was for one of them to *want* to interview
him for the job, and no amount of self-serving prompting on
his part was going to get them there.

Of course, I didn't have much control over NFL coaching
opportunities. Okay, I had none. And so I just kept making sure
Tony knew I believed in him and was 100 percent behind him.
I also reminded him that he had a good job doing what he loved

as an assistant coach and that we had each other, a wonderful family, and a God who loved us and would never fail us.

As far as I was concerned, a big part of my job description during those years of waiting was to support and encourage Tony. He has also been my chief supporter in times of difficulty, disappointment, and heartache.

That's the lesson the apostle Paul paints in today's verses. We've all heard these words read at weddings—and for good reason. It's a worthy mission statement for our marriages. Love is not always sunshine and rainbows, but it is always patient and kind—especially in the difficult times. Love rejoices when the truth wins out, and I knew that one day my husband's coaching ability would land him a top coaching job. In the meantime, I was going to do all I could do to help him keep his chin up and realize how special he was. After all, "love never gives up, never loses faith, is always hopeful, and endures through every circumstance."

Adventure Application: Take a moment to reconsider what love is and what it is not, according to today's Scripture passage. Discuss which one attribute you most want to develop so you can love your spouse better.

day 54
AS TIME GOES BY

CORE PRACTICE #47:
Cherish every moment with family members.

....

A time to cry and a time to laugh.
  A time to grieve and a time to dance.
—ECCLESIASTES 3:4

TONY

I've rarely been happier than when Lauren and our children were finally able to join me in Indianapolis in 2003. After a year and a half apart, we would finally be living in the same house again. Yet like any long-distance move, this one brought a few temporary inconveniences. For instance, for a day or two all of our stuff was boxed up—including the kids' toys.

So when I wanted to find something to do with eleven-year-old Eric, I grabbed a roll of tape and one of our brooms and asked if he wanted to play "tape baseball." That's when I realized that my son can really hit!

A few days later, I asked Eric during a casual conversation, "What was the best time you ever had with me?"

His eyes lit up and he said, "Dad, the greatest time I ever had with you was beating you in tape baseball, 22 to 3."

"Really?" I said. "That was better than being on the sidelines with me? Better than going to the Pro Bowl together? Better than catching passes from Kurt Warner? Why?"

"Because it was the last thing we did together."

Wow. Talk about an eye-opening moment. What matters most to our kids aren't the flashy things; it's what we do with them every day. Of course, the same is true for parents: Our best memories aren't of great achievements at work or any award. They are the moments we spent with loved ones.

I appreciate how one Scripture so often sheds light on another. Perhaps the best-known section of Ecclesiastes (where today's verse is found) points out that there is a time for everything under heaven.[8] The apostle James reminds us why that's so important to remember: "How do you know what your life will be like tomorrow? Your life is like the morning fog—it's here a little while, then it's gone" (James 4:14).

And so, might I add, are our children. We assume we're going to have many "tomorrows" with them, but we can't count on that. We need to take advantage of the time that God has given us today. Eric and our daughter Tiara are now living on their own. The days of playing tape baseball with our son or cheering on Tiara at her cross country races are over. I'm so thankful I didn't miss them.

Adventure Application: Spend a few minutes today reminiscing about some treasured times spent with either your kids or with other family members or friends. You might even ask your kids what their favorite family memory is. Prepare to be surprised!

day 55
FAMILY MATTERS

CORE PRACTICE #48:
Treat your kids' sports and other activities as being just as important as anything else on your family calendar.

Unless the LORD builds a house,
the work of the builders is wasted.
Unless the LORD protects a city,
guarding it with sentries will do no good.
It is useless for you to work so hard
from early morning until late at night,
anxiously working for food to eat;
for God gives rest to his loved ones.

—PSALM 127:1-2

Lauren

In our kitchen, not far from our master calendar, hangs what we call our family prayer board. This whiteboard is a place for every member of our family to write down their prayer concerns and requests. We often date each comment—and sometimes even add a brief note about how the prayer was answered. In the midst of reminders to pray for family health issues and travel concerns, our kids write down requests like, "Pray for me. I'm going to try out for the track team."

This is just one of the tools Tony and I use to teach our kids about the importance and power of prayer. It also reminds them that their activities and concerns are just as important to us as our own.

Over the years, Tony and I have learned the importance

of guarding our priorities—including those of our kids. We talk about them with our family a great deal. We also commit them to God in prayer before less important activities become "urgent." The reality, like it or not, is that we tend to do a better job at honoring our commitments when we write them on our calendar. So it follows that we should make sure we schedule those more important priorities of our lives.

The number one priority for each of us should be the Lord—following Him, spending time with Him, seeking His will. Number two should be our spouse and number three, our children. All the other activities of life fall somewhere below.

That's why, whenever our children have concerts, school functions, or athletic events, Tony and I want them to see our faces in the stands or in the auditorium. Whether they win or lose, perform well or not, our presence tells them plainly and simply, without words, that we love and care for them and that they are important.

So when our son Eric played football at the University of Oregon, the Ducks' fall football games became family events for us. We all have traveled cross-country to watch Eric play, and we knew that he appreciated the support of the whole family.

We have made similar commitments and sacrifices to be at Jordan's field trips, Jade's sixth grade track meets, Justin's T-ball games, and Jason's five-and-under soccer games. We want our kids to know that their events are worthy of our prayer and attendance—and just as important as supporting Dad when he coached at the Super Bowl.

Adventure Application: What can you do this week to let your kids know that their activities matter as much to you as your own?

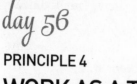
day 56

PRINCIPLE 4

WORK AS A TEAM.

....

UNCOMMON WISDOM

A house is built by wisdom
  and becomes strong through good sense.
Through knowledge its rooms are filled
  with all sorts of precious riches and valuables.

—PROVERBS 24:3-4

UNCOMMON PRACTICE

Take a few moments to select one of this week's practices to explore further. The related Adventure Application appears just below each practice. If you'd prefer to come up with a different way of living out that practice this week, feel free to discuss what that might look like.

- *Establish household routines to cut down on confusion and stress, but prioritize relationships over structure.* How well do you and your spouse balance the need for both household order and relationship building? Which comes easier for you? What is one step you can take this week to strengthen the area that doesn't come as naturally?

- *Stay connected through date nights and joint activities.* Do you have a date night scheduled sometime in the next month? If not, take a few minutes to discuss a fun activity you could do together. Then get out your calendar and schedule it.

- *Don't rush into making major decisions.*
Is your family facing a difficult decision? If so, are you waiting on God and listening for His voice? If you're not in decision-making mode now, how can you prepare yourself so you're ready the next time you face a major turning point?

- *Consistently demonstrate support for your spouse.*
Take a moment to reconsider what love is and what it is not, according to today's Scripture passage. Discuss which one attribute you most want to develop so you can love your spouse better.

- *Cherish every moment with family members.*
Spend a few minutes today reminiscing about some treasured times spent with either your kids or with other family members or friends. You might even ask your kids what their favorite family memory is. Prepare to be surprised!

- *Treat your kids' sports and other activities as being just as important as anything else on your family calendar.*
What can you do this week to let your kids know that their activities matter as much to you as your own?

UNCOMMON PRAYER

Take a few minutes to discuss any praises and needs you'd like to bring to God as a couple. Then, in addition to praying about those things, use one or more of the following prayer prompts to ask for God's strength and wisdom as you seek to work as a team.

Take turns praising God for at least one specific way your partner served you this week—whether it was by giving you a warm smile, a word of encouragement, or practical help around the house.

Confess any times you've taken each other for granted or neglected to thank your spouse for his or her care and support.

Ask the Holy Spirit to guide you as you make decisions—large or small—and to direct you both so that you reach mutual agreement.

day 57
COMMITTED

CORE PRACTICE #49: Commit to stay together, no matter what.

"Haven't you read the Scriptures?" Jesus replied. "They record that from the beginning 'God made them male and female.' And he said, "'This explains why a man leaves his father and mother and is joined to his wife, and the two are united into one.' Since they are no longer two but one, let no one split apart what God has joined together."

—MATTHEW 19:4-6

TONY

Lauren and I feel incredibly fortunate that we can point to our parents as our role models. Growing up, we seldom noticed our parents' struggles, but we figure not every moment went as they had hoped it would. And we are pretty sure that neither Lauren's parents nor mine agreed on every decision. But we saw that they took seriously the vows they had made to each other. They had made a promise they couldn't and wouldn't walk away from, no matter what difficulties they faced.

So why does holding a marriage together seem so much harder these days? After all, our parents weren't immune from adversities. I think one reason is that our parents chose to look at life through the eyes of faith, rather than fear. They refused to live in fear and uncertainty, paralyzed by wondering, *But what if this happens? What if we disagree? What if we struggle financially?* They knew that no matter what they faced, God would walk them through it.

Many married couples today seem to focus on their circumstances and their feelings. They also try building their relationship on the shaky foundation of cultural expectations. They want to fit in, to be accepted, to achieve the American dream. The problem is, our feelings, our circumstances, and even our cultural standards are constantly shifting.

Depending on the survey you look at, one-third to one-half of all marriages end in divorce. Many states have made it too easy to separate and divorce, passing laws that enable couples to dissolve their vows simply by claiming that the marriage is "irretrievably broken." Whatever that means.

That's the bad news. The good news is that God designed something better. As Jesus says in this passage, God puts marriages together to be permanent, and we can't let anything pull ours apart. When we make such a commitment, Christ will be the glue that holds us together. A strong marriage provides stability and support, not only for a couple but for their children and the wider community. It nurtures a lasting love that can endure and grow in the midst of the inevitable disappointments that life brings. Whenever Lauren and I face difficulties or feel any distance from each other, the commitment we made to each other years ago begins to draw us back together.

That doesn't mean it's always easy. In fact, in our own strength and given our own inherent selfishness, marriage is just too hard. That's why an uncommon marriage is one in which a husband and wife place God at the center. They look to Christ and to the Bible to guide them. Their goal is a permanent bond that endures through anything. That's a simple statement, but it's a radical one. It's uncommon.

Adventure Application: You learned about commitment and marriage from your parents. What other influences—media, your friends, or the wider culture—have shaped your views? How do those messages square with Jesus' words in today's Scripture?

day 58
BEFORE BABY MAKES THREE

CORE PRACTICE #50:
Spend time, if possible, getting to know each other before starting a family.

....

Let your wife be a fountain of blessing for you.
  Rejoice in the wife of your youth.

—PROVERBS 5:18

Lauren

Tony and I had known each other for just eleven months before our wedding. Though we'd agreed to meet only because my pastor kept urging us to do so, our relationship quickly took off once we realized that we shared a common faith, as well as similar values and interests. Before long, we began thinking about whether or not to get married.

Obviously, we chose marriage.

So though we advise married couples to consider waiting before having kids, we realize that their situation may be different from ours. Some spouses gain stepchildren when they marry. Others discover they're expecting shortly after the honeymoon. Some people are much older when they marry and plan to start families right away. Every child is a blessing, and his or her arrival should be celebrated.

Not only that, but some couples know each other much better than Tony and I did when we married. Many meet while attending high school or college together. That gives them the opportunity to get to know each other as friends and classmates first. Others have long courtships while they finish their schooling or begin their careers.

Tony and I, however, appreciated taking time after our wedding to get to know each other even better. That's when we began to really talk about our vision for our lives, our marriage, and our family. Those two and a half years together, before our first child, Tiara, was born, helped us build a strong foundation. We were able to travel, build friendships with other couples, and find common interests. We enjoyed developing our careers, and we bought our first home together which put us closer to my family—and a support system—before our daughter was born. Most important, we began to incorporate Bible study and prayer as normal parts of our routines, both as a couple and within our church.

Waiting a while didn't stunt the size of our family either. We have nine children now, including six at home. Tony and I often remark that our life is a whirlwind, with never-ending homework, music lessons, athletic practices and games, sleepovers, church youth group activities, and dance lessons on our schedules.

And we love it. But it doesn't always leave time just for us. So it was wise that we had a couple of years alone as a young couple before we began to have children.

Adventure Application: Deciding when and if to have children is just one of many decisions married couples must make. If you were to recommend one choice you and your spouse made (or wish you had made) early on to establish a strong foundation for your marriage, what would it be?

day 59
SHARED SACRIFICE

CORE PRACTICE #51:
Be willing to sacrifice to support your spouse's passion.

....

Live a life filled with love, following the example of Christ. He loved
us and offered himself as a sacrifice for us. —EPHESIANS 5:2

TONY

I like to think that I have sacrificed for Lauren and our family
throughout our marriage. I believe I have, and I think Lauren
would agree.

Yet here's the plain, painful, and honest truth: For twenty-
seven of the thirty-plus years we've been married, I was a professional football coach. That means for nearly three decades, I was
away from home for summer training camps, college scouting
trips, and weekend football games played in another city. If you
figure each training camp was about a month long, that alone
meant I was away from the family for more than two years just
to prepare my teams for another season!

My career resulted in twenty-seven years of missed quality
time and special moments with Lauren and our kids. Our family moved five times to five different cities during that twenty-
seven-year period, which meant uprooting Lauren and our
children and disrupting the relationships they had developed.

The real sacrifice during those years came not from me but
from Lauren. She understood that coaching was not only my
job, not only something I was good at, but also something I
loved. She wanted to help me follow my passion in life, so she
took every opportunity to make certain she could enjoy doing

it along with me. Whether traveling with me to away games or helping our football teams become a force for good in our communities, Lauren was with me every step of my career. Yet it required sacrifices from her too numerous to recount. Sacrifices that I appreciated and that caused me to love her even more.

The only person Lauren can't outdo when it comes to putting aside her own preferences for me is Christ. Of course, He did the same for her and for you. It's only when we live out of gratitude for His indescribable gift that we can live and love each other "with one mind and purpose."

For years Lauren knew that between July and February, my schedule was mapped out, which often meant that she would carry the responsibilities at home on her own. So when people ask me whether I have any desire to return to coaching, I have to say, no, I wouldn't go back. Much as I enjoyed the challenges and the relationships with my players and staff, I appreciate being able to turn down a speaking request because it's my daughter's birthday and I want to spend the day with her.

And I like that today I can return the favor, whether by supporting Lauren as she trains for triathlons or by taking the kids to and from school and doctors' appointments.

But I do so knowing that my efforts to help her don't compare to the sacrifices she made for me all those years—which may be one reason why I'm more open to taking her out on the dance floor for a spin every now and again.

Adventure Application: Where can you do better at sacrificing to help support something your spouse really loves and wants to do? Find a way to do that this week.

day 60
CHANGING FOR THE BETTER

CORE PRACTICE #52:
Be sensitive and considerate to your spouse during transitions.

....

So now I am giving you a new commandment: Love each other. Just as I have loved you, you should love each other. Your love for one another will prove to the world that you are my disciples. —JOHN 13:34-35

Lauren

Change. It's not for the squeamish.

Most people—me included—don't look forward to having to go through it. Tony is a strong, adaptable, optimistic person, but transitions are hard for him too. Change is difficult because we are moving from the certain to the uncertain, wanting to believe it will be for good but not really knowing what the next season will bring.

Tony's chosen career path resulted in a lot of change for us and our children. Tony admitted it was always a little easier for him to adapt than it was for us, and I suspect he's right. Because he recognized the adjustments we had to make, I'm grateful that he did all he could to help us get acclimated as quickly as possible in our new surroundings.

For example, when he left the Kansas City Chiefs to take a promotion and become defensive coordinator with the Minnesota Vikings, we all faced big changes. But Tony's new job thrust him back into a familiar setting: The faces of many of the fifty-three players and fifteen coaches may have been new to him, but he already had a relationship with his boss, Denny Green, as well as several of the other staff members. In addition, he had long workdays doing what he loved to keep him busy. The children and I, on the other hand, had left a neighborhood we'd grown to love in Kansas City, not to mention our friends at church and within the Chiefs' organization.

As is the case with most moves, building relationships and finding friends took some time—especially since we arrived in Minnesota in the off-season. As excited as Tony was to be back in the city where he'd been a football standout in college, he realized that this wasn't an easy transition for the rest of us. Particularly during that first winter when our home was surrounded by snowdrifts, Tony tried to make things better. He introduced me to other coaches' wives. We looked together for a church where we could develop new friendships. He agreed to go on an end-of-school camping trip with two other families the kids and I had gotten to know through their elementary school.

The bottom line for Tony was this: Even though he and his career had been the impetus for this change, he needed to focus on us and our needs. We were the ones adrift.

Tony did. And we got through it.

And, yes, the snow eventually melted.

Adventure Application: Are you currently going through a period of change, or are you looking ahead to a transition in the future? Talk to each other about it. Plan what you can do to help each other and your children with any change.

day 61
LESSONS IN GRIEF

CORE PRACTICE #53: Expect that life will bring some difficult times; don't let them pull you away from your spouse.

....

I am convinced that nothing can ever separate us from God's love. Neither death nor life, neither angels nor demons, neither our fears for today nor our worries about tomorrow—not even the powers of hell can separate us from God's love. No power in the sky above or in the earth below—indeed, nothing in all creation will ever be able to separate us from the love of God that is revealed in Christ Jesus our Lord. —ROMANS 8:37-39

Lauren

The sorrow and pain Tony and I experienced that December night was indescribable. I would never want anyone else to have to go through it—there is simply no way to understand the sense of loss that comes crashing down in a moment like that.

That's what happened when we received a phone call in the middle of the night three days before Christmas 2005. When the phone rang, I handed it to Tony because any late-night phone calls we received were usually related to the Colts. This one wasn't. Instead, the caller on the other end of the line was a Tampa policeman who told us the devastating news that our second-oldest child, Jamie, had taken his life.

Shock led to disbelief, and then to deep-seated sorrow. How could this be? It simply made no sense. Jamie was a tender-hearted, compassionate young man who was always making friends, especially with those who needed a friend. It was an unexpected moment of darkness for us.

The outpouring of love and support for us that we soon received, however, was real and overwhelming. During those first few days, Tony and I held tightly to each other as never before. And, looking back, I know that making prayer and regular communication between us such an important part of our marriage before then enabled us to navigate the deep waters of grief. But even though we knew Jamie's faith assured his place in heaven, our journey wasn't easy.

We learned that we grieved differently and that grief doesn't operate on a timetable or a schedule. Some days Tony would be having a good day and I wasn't. That might be reversed the next day. Yet no matter how we were feeling, we continued to cling to our faith in God and our unwavering belief that not only was He there, but that as we wept, He wept with us.

We never felt separated from each other, and even more important, we never felt separated from the Lord. In the inspirational Scripture above, the apostle Paul makes it abundantly clear to us all—no matter what we go through, no matter what happens to us or around us, no matter what happens to those we love and those who love us, nothing will ever be able to separate us—or them—from the love of God found in Christ Jesus our Lord. That is clear through what Christ did for all of us on the cross—which forever connects us with Him and provides us with eternal access to the God of all creation.

And His word to us always: Love each other. Cling to Him. In good times and not-so-good times. Forever and ever.

Adventure Application: We hope you're not facing anything now that is causing you sorrow or pain. The reality of life is that eventually we all will face a heartbreaking experience that brings us to a point of despair. Be ready, cling to Him, and hold fast to each other. Stay close and remember how much He loves you and all of His children.

day 62

FOR BETTER, FOR WORSE

CORE PRACTICE #54:
Affirm and express love to your spouse—especially when he or she is going through tough times.

Share each other's burdens, and in this way obey the law of Christ. If you think you are too important to help someone, you are only fooling yourself. You are not that important. —GALATIANS 6:2-3

Lauren

Sometimes the wives of football players and coaches wryly joke among themselves that "NFL" must be short for "not for long." That's because trades, cuts, and firings are pretty common. All kidding aside, being forced to leave a team is never easy.

Throughout the 2001 season, I lived with an unsettling feeling that, short of a Super Bowl win, my husband's days with the Bucs might soon be over. Rather than the close, friendly relationship we'd had with the team's owners in previous years, they had become businesslike and seemed to exclude us from decision making. I realized they might be severing ties because they planned to move in a different direction. Tony and I had to prepare for that as well.

Because Tony tends to take people at their word—and the team's management had assured him he had nothing to worry about—he brushed off my concerns. He remained focused on winning games and bringing out the best in his players. Given Tony's optimism and my realism, I guess it's not surprising that we perceived the situation differently!

The first big blow to our family that season actually had

nothing to do with the Bucs. Just after the New Year, Tony's mother died. That was a big loss to Tony, although the many tributes from her former high school students were a comfort to both of us. They also reminded us of what really matters in life.

Less than two weeks later, the Bucs were scheduled to fly to Philadelphia for a playoff game against the Eagles. That same day, the *St. Petersburg Times* ran a story that leaked information from a team insider that said Tony would be fired if they didn't win the game on Saturday. Tony planned to ask one of the team owners about it on the flight to Philadelphia, but for the first time, the owners weren't on the team plane. Tony was finally ready to concede that he might not be returning to the Bucs after the season ended.

And so, after the Bucs lost to the Eagles that Saturday night, neither of us was very surprised when Tony was summoned to a brief meeting with the Glazers—just long enough for them to tell him he was fired.

Tony told me he was ready to move on; I hurt for him and felt let down. But I was also reminded that we share a special bond with our spouses that enables us to "share one another's burdens" in a unique and powerful way. I couldn't take away Tony's hurt, but I could let him know I was there for him and he wasn't carrying that disappointment alone.

When Tony had taken the job in Tampa, we believed God would reward us if we led the team in a way that honored Him. Being fired was not the outcome we expected, but it was the answer we got. Thankfully, it wasn't the end of the story.

Adventure Application: Paul calls us to pay attention and to express our love to each other always, especially during those most difficult moments. How can you do that this week for your spouse? And next week?

day 63

PRINCIPLE 5
PRACTICE COMMITTED LOVE.

UNCOMMON WISDOM

Then the LORD God made a woman from the rib, and he brought her to the man.

"At last!" the man exclaimed.
"This one is bone from my bone,
*   and flesh from my flesh!*
She will be called 'woman,'
*   because she was taken from 'man.'"*

This explains why a man leaves his father and mother and is joined to his wife, and the two are united into one.
—GENESIS 2:22-24

UNCOMMON PRACTICE

Take a few moments to select one of this week's practices to explore further. The related Adventure Application appears just below each practice. If you'd prefer to come up with a different way of living out that practice this week, feel free to discuss what that might look like.

- *Commit to stay together, no matter what.*
  You learned about commitment and marriage from your parents. What other influences—media, your friends, or the wider culture—have shaped your views? How do those messages square with Jesus' words in today's Scripture?

- *Spend time, if possible, getting to know each other before starting a family.*
  Deciding when and if to have children is just one of many decisions married couples must make. If you were to recommend one choice you and your spouse made (or wish you had made) early on to establish a strong foundation for your marriage, what would it be?

- *Be willing to sacrifice to support your spouse's passion.*
  Where can you do better at sacrificing to help support something your spouse really loves and wants to do? Find a way to do that this week.

- *Be sensitive and considerate to your spouse during transitions.*
  Are you currently going through a period of change, or are you looking ahead to a transition in the future? Talk to each other about it. Plan what each of you can do to help the other and your children with any change.

- *Expect that life will bring some difficult times; don't let them pull you away from your spouse.*
  We hope you're not facing anything now that is causing you sorrow or pain. The reality of life is that eventually we all will face a heartbreaking experience that brings us to a point of despair. Be ready, and cling to Him, and hold fast to each other. Stay close and remember how much He loves you and all of His children.

- *Affirm and express love to your spouse—especially when he or she is going through tough times.*
  Paul calls us to pay attention and to express our love to each other always, including those most difficult

moments. How can you do that this week for your spouse? And next week?

UNCOMMON PRAYER

Take a few minutes to discuss any praises and needs you'd like to bring to God as a couple. Then, in addition to praying about those things, use one or more of the following prayer prompts to ask for God to deepen your love for and commitment to each other.

Praise God for His unconditional love for you, along with His promise never to leave or forsake you (see Deuteronomy 31:6).

Confess anything—whether resentment, mistrust, fear, disagreements, conflict—that is hampering your ability to love each other as you would like. Ask God to begin to soften both of your hearts so you can be more tender with each other.

Intercede for family members who do not yet know the Father's love for them. Ask God to show you one way you might model His love to them in the coming week.

day 64
ALL IN

CORE PRACTICE #55:
Be willing to step up and do a little more than usual when the situation requires it.

....

This is the message you have heard from the beginning: We should love one another. . . . We know what real love is because Jesus gave up his life for us. So we also ought to give up our lives for our brothers and sisters. —1 JOHN 3:11, 16

Lauren

Some people talk about meeting a spouse "halfway" or somehow splitting duties to be fair. But this attitude may not be the best. Even the term *equally yoked* can lead to the wrong idea—that marriage is a fifty-fifty proposition.

It's not. Yes, compromising and sharing responsibilities both have a role in a relationship. After all, marriage is a partnership, and both spouses need to come together to shoulder the duties, responsibilities, and decision making. But the *relationship itself* is not a meeting in the middle; it's a total sellout by each person.

Marriage is not a fifty-fifty commitment. Tony and I learned long ago that marriage requires a 100 percent commitment from each partner. As Frank Sinatra sang long ago, "When somebody loves you, it's no good unless he loves you all the way . . ."[9]

That's also the lesson of Christ's love for each of us. After John wrote his Gospel account of Christ's life and earthly ministry, he went on to write the letters we know as 1, 2, and 3 John, as well as Revelation. In those books he elaborates on lessons he learned from Christ and the Holy Spirit. In today's

Scripture passage, John reminds us that "We know what real love is because Jesus gave up his life for us."

Christ gave us every bit of Himself because He loved us. He gave us His body, blood, breath—everything—for our salvation and to fulfill the prophecies of Scripture and the promises of His Father for us. John then goes a little further in the next verse when he reminds us that "we also ought to give up our lives for our brothers and sisters." And there is no better or more appropriate place to start than in our marriage.

Sometimes the total commitment we show our spouses goes unnoticed by the outside world; at other times, we need to take a public stand. For instance, our family went to every one of Tony's home games and to most of the away games. We didn't stay just for the game but always waited for Tony after the game outside the locker room. As a result, we were often subjected to the criticism of fans—the opposing team's, and sometimes even our own, depending on the outcome of the game. But we were there 100 percent of the time—and Tony knew he could count on us being there. When he came out of that locker room, he knew he'd see our faces.

Likewise, your spouse needs to know that he or she will always see your face and feel your support—100 percent of the time.

Adventure Application: Marriage is not a fifty-fifty proposition. It requires a 100 percent commitment from each spouse. What can you do this week to begin to demonstrate that you understand and are committed to that in your marriage?

day 65
SEALING YOUR LOVE

CORE PRACTICE #56: Seek to keep your romance alive, but be aware that it's normal for feelings to fluctuate and change over time; don't let unrealistic expectations of constant romance diminish your commitment to—or satisfaction with—your relationship.

Place me like a seal over your heart,
*   like a seal on your arm.*
For love is as strong as death,
*   its jealousy as enduring as the grave. . . .*
Many waters cannot quench love,
*   nor can rivers drown it.*

—SONG OF SONGS 8:6-7

TONY

I can still remember, before Lauren and I were married, how my heart would skip a beat whenever I anticipated seeing her coming around the corner of a building or into a room.

In the years that followed, our love strengthened, moving beyond those intense "feelings" to greater affection, respect, and support. In some ways, maturing love is more difficult because it moves past spontaneous emotion to intentional action. Yet this kind of love is more solid—like the "seal over your heart" that the young woman narrating the portion of Scripture above describes. In her day, seals were used as a form of identification or to show ownership. Wealthy people wore rings with a raised seal etched into them. When they pressed the face of the ring into soft wax, they created a seal that literally sealed the deal.

By the time the Colts offered me a head coaching position

in 2002, Lauren and I had weathered many storms and knew our love was enduring. We saw this coaching opportunity as one orchestrated by God. Taking the job, however, came at a price that felt costly at times to our marriage and family.

Lauren and I decided that I would go by myself for the first year and a half. She and the children would stay in Tampa until our daughter Tiara, then a high school junior, graduated with her class the following year.

And so that's what we worked out. We made it a point to talk by phone every night, although being in different time zones sometimes made it tough to connect with the kids. Our older children knew the sacrifice we were making, but they still missed me, and I missed them. Our younger ones didn't understand why I couldn't be with them, which made it really tough to be apart.

We wouldn't recommend this arrangement for newly married couples or those with shaky relationships. It's not ideal for anyone. However, by then we'd been married for twenty years and our marriage was strong and stable, so we felt we could make it work. And we did.

Throughout this period, our love for each other continued to mature. That's what happens in a God-ordained marriage. Love changes and grows. It doesn't go away because the feelings change; it simply gets stronger.

After two decades of marriage, Lauren and I felt confident that even a thousand-mile separation couldn't quench our love. And, by God's grace, we were right.

Adventure Application: This week, sit down with your spouse and discuss how your love for each other has changed and grown stronger through the years. Take a few minutes to express gratitude to God and to each other.

day 66
WEIGH YOUR WORDS

CORE PRACTICE #57:
Show the world that you are your partner's greatest fan.

....

Her children stand and bless her.
  Her husband praises her:
"There are many virtuous and capable women in the world,
  but you surpass them all!"
—PROVERBS 31:28-29

TONY

I don't know if you have ever witnessed something like this. But the few times I have seen it convinced me I should never do it to Lauren.

Occasionally when we have been to gatherings with other couples, I've heard a husband or a wife begin to "joke" about their spouse. This person tells everyone about something stupid, silly, or unbelievably inappropriate he or she had just done. The only reason for telling us had to be to get a laugh at the expense of the spouse—the husband or wife who was to be loved and protected above all others. The speaker often softened the blow a bit by prefacing the remark with, "I'm only kidding," and reminding everyone that their spouse had a good sense of humor and could take it.

Occasionally such joking is okay, I suppose, but over time it can damage your spouse's sense of self-worth, as well as the bond of trust, respect, and admiration that should exist within a marriage.

Today's verses from Proverbs 31, a portion of Scripture

usually referred to as "A Wife of Noble Character," suggests a different way to treat one's spouse. Though written by a husband, these words reflect the way Lauren has treated me all the years of our marriage—with respect, trust, and praise to others. She has never ridiculed or made fun of me in front of others— even, or especially, in the name of "only joking" or "kidding."

Instead, Lauren has always been my biggest fan. She has taught our children by her example how to appreciate me and applaud me for what I do each day of my life. For years, Lauren came to all my games. Win or lose, she was always there and always vocal in her support of the team and me. Always. She never criticized me for a mistake, either outright or by telling a "joke" at my expense. I have always tried to do the same— supporting her privately and publicly for all she does. Certainly I would never resort to ridicule her in the name of good-natured ribbing.

After the many years she has cheered me on from the sidelines, I was grateful last year to be able to support her at a sporting event. She was competing in her first triathlon, a sprint triathlon held at Fort Desoto Park in St. Petersburg, Florida. The kids and I had such fun taking pictures and yelling for her at the end of the race as she crossed the finish line.

As husbands, we don't have to wait for our wives to do something special like a triathlon, however. We need to be their biggest fan every day. We always need to be the ones encouraging, lifting, edifying, and affirming our wives' place and purpose in this world. The same thing is true for wives. From the standpoint of us husbands, I can tell you that when Lauren supports me, my sense of well-being and accomplishment is immediately elevated.

So the next time you're tempted to talk about your spouse to anyone else, I urge you to weigh your comment first. Ask yourself, *Do the words sound as if they're coming from my spouse's biggest fan?* If not, maybe they shouldn't be spoken at all. Or better yet, why not replace them with a statement like, "There are many virtuous and capable people in the world, but you surpass them all!" In your own words, of course!

Adventure Application: Look for an opportunity to say something positive about your wife or husband this week, both privately and publicly. If you're tempted to criticize him or her, take a minute to weigh your words before you speak.

day 67
ALL IN THE FAMILY

CORE PRACTICE #58:
Care for the needs of your spouse's family as an expression of your love for your husband or wife.

....

But those who won't care for their relatives, especially those in their own household, have denied the true faith. Such people are worse than unbelievers. —1 TIMOTHY 5:8

Lauren

When we commit to love, honor, and obey our spouse until "death us do part," our minds and hearts are usually focused directly, and only, upon each other.

That's how it should be.

And yet we need to understand that when two people exchange vows, they each also double the size of their extended family. As the apostle Paul makes clear in the Scripture passage above, these are people they need to get to know better and to love, in all settings, no matter what.

We should view these new relationships as a privilege and another of God's gifts to us through our marriage. The opportunity to care for them, to help them in moments of need, and to provide companionship can no doubt be challenging, yet we need to view these relationships through God's eyes.

Often, it's our parents who most need our help as they age. For Tony and me, this first became an issue in 2000, when his mother's health really started to decline. After breaking her hip while visiting us, she was largely confined to a wheelchair. I was concerned and told Tony, "If anything happens to your dad, we need to have her come and stay here." Though his mom died the following year—several years before his dad's death—I discovered that my commitment to care for his mom meant a great deal to Tony.

Likewise, his commitment to honor and help my mom, Doris, is a source of great joy for me. I've always been very close to her, but our relationship has grown even closer since my dad died. Doing things to help my mom is a blessing for our entire family, and we love to have her come visit and spend time with us. Last Christmas we decided to purchase a big flat-screen television for her to enjoy in her home. I really don't know who felt best when it was delivered: Mom, because of the gift; me, as I saw the joy that this gift brought to her; or Tony, knowing I felt so good about doing something special for my mother.

My eyes were only on Tony on our wedding day, but I'm grateful that we both willingly extended that love to our family members who had helped make us who we were. What a privilege.

Adventure Application: Do you need to reach out to help someone in your spouse's family? Don't wait to be asked. Offer to do something for that family member, and then make sure you follow through. Not only will you be loving as Christ commands us to do, but your spouse will be grateful and feel loved.

day 68
IN FOCUS

CORE PRACTICE #59:
Build an uncommon marriage by staying focused on each other and allowing God to lead you.

....

Teach me to do your will,
for you are my God.
May your gracious Spirit lead me forward
on a firm footing.

—PSALM 143:10

TONY

Rick Warren started his book *The Purpose Driven Life* with this phrase: "It's not about you."

He's absolutely right. Despite the fact that we often wake up with ourselves first and foremost on our minds—it's not about us.

Instead, it's all about God.

It's all about what He is doing in our lives and the world. Because Lauren and I have been involved with the NFL, many people imagine that our lives are more glamorous or trouble free than theirs. Can I let you in on a secret? The sources of our stress may be different, but everyone struggles to balance their commitments at home and at work, and we all face challenges that can work against our marriage.

Incredibly, as David makes clear in today's verses, we only need to ask the Lord, and He will teach us His will and lead us forward. The key, though, is to keep the focus off ourselves and on God. That's why prayer is such an important part of my life.

I need His help to turn the focus from me and my concerns to my heavenly Father and His ability to keep me on the right path.

For instance, I still struggle with the tension that comes from wanting to be home for my kids, but at the same time, needing to honor commitments that require me to be in another city. That's why I'm constantly asking the Lord to direct me so that when we're together, I'm doing what's most important to Lauren and our kids. When I am home, I've learned I need to zero in and make sure I'm doing what matters most for them. It's not necessarily what my kids want to do either. Sometimes it means quizzing them as they're preparing for a test. Yet whatever we do together, I want to let them know they're important. It's really not about me.

That's one reason Lauren and I wrote *Uncommon Marriage*, as well as this devotional. We want to show you that when you and your spouse keep Christ at the center of your marriage and remain committed to each other, you can make it through all the storms of life. In an uncommon marriage, you don't focus on your own needs, but you seek to honor your partner's needs as they follow God's leading. That's why understanding God's will for your life may involve, at times, working harder to understand God's will for your *spouse's* life.

And ironically, I've discovered that I am most fulfilled and content when I remember it's not about me and, instead, seek the good of my family members.

Adventure Application: As stress piles up, it can be more difficult to keep the focus off ourselves and our own problems. Take a few minutes to honestly consider where you are when it comes to turning your concerns over to God and leaning on your spouse for the support you need. Then bring any frustrations you feel to God in prayer.

day 69
KEEPING THE FAITH

CORE PRACTICE #60:
**Rest in the assurance that God, who promises never to leave
or forsake you, knows what's ahead for your family.**

....

*But Moses told the people, "Don't be afraid. Just stand still and watch
the LORD rescue you today. The Egyptians you see today will never be
seen again. The LORD himself will fight for you. Just stay calm."*
—EXODUS 14:13-14

TONY

October 6, 2003 was a night I'll never forget. I was coaching the
Indianapolis Colts, and we were playing the defending Super
Bowl Champion Tampa Bay Buccaneers on Monday Night
Football—on my birthday! To add to the drama, the Bucs had
fired me before the previous season, and this would be the first
time I would be back in the stadium where I had coached for
so long. But now we were the opposition and the Bucs had a
great team, led by the number-one ranked defense in the NFL.

The game obviously meant a lot to me personally. Lauren
and the kids would be in the stands cheering as loud as they
could, but it was going to be a huge challenge. I prayed that
our team would play its best and that we could come out with
a victory. I had faith that God would answer. However, as the
game developed, it became harder to maintain that faith. We
quickly fell behind 21–0, and nothing went right for us early
on. In the second half we played a little better, but with less
than five minutes to play, we still trailed by twenty-one points.
At that moment, things appeared hopeless.

I think I felt a little of what Moses must have been feeling, standing on the banks of the Red Sea after leading the Israelites out of Egypt. Moses knew God would sustain him and the Israelites. No doubt many times before, Moses had silently pondered the truth that he would eventually say to the Israelites: "The LORD himself will fight for you. Just stay calm" (Exodus 14:14).

After all, Moses had seen God act in mighty ways from the time He selected him to deliver His people from the oppressive hand of Pharaoh to that very day when Moses led them out of Egypt into the desert, heading toward the Promised Land. But now, just as they arrived at the shore of the Red Sea, they faced a new danger—one that threatened their very lives. Their path forward was blocked by the sea, and all they could see behind them was Pharaoh's army and chariots in full pursuit. No wonder the Israelites lost heart. They were stuck between their past and the deep waters ahead. Now what?

Amid this frantic situation, Moses had to deal with the Israelites complaining. Naturally, they were worried. Having reached the end of his own wisdom, ability, and expertise, Moses determined to focus on the God whom he trusted.

So Moses told the people to trust God. "The LORD himself will fight for you. Just stay calm." And something occurred that no one expected. After hearing from God, Moses stretched out his hand and staff—and God parted the waters of the Red Sea so the Israelites could walk to safety.

The Red Sea didn't open up for the Colts in Tampa that night, but a miracle did happen—something that had never been done before in the history of the NFL. We scored three touchdowns in the last four and a half minutes to tie the game. We then kicked a field goal in overtime to complete the comeback victory.

We have all found ourselves standing on the shore of a "Red

Sea" with threatening circumstances all around us. We've all faced what appear to be insurmountable obstacles and challenges, knowing we've reached the limits of our own wisdom, ability, and expertise.

In such moments, we need to remember that God is still there. We can stay calm, even when we don't have it all figured out or under control, remembering that the Lord will continue to fight for us. As we were in the locker room after the game, that's what we were thinking—*What a remarkable thing the Lord has done tonight!*

Adventure Application: What are you facing that you can't seem to see through or over or around into the next day? Remember that God hasn't gone anywhere; He will continue to fight for you as you wonder and stand ready to move ahead. What can you do today to keep that truth in mind—and just stay calm?

day 70

PRINCIPLE 5
PRACTICE COMMITTED LOVE.

UNCOMMON WISDOM

Let your wife be a fountain of blessing for you. . . . May you always be captivated by her love. —PROVERBS 5:18-19

UNCOMMON PRACTICE

Take a few moments to select one of this week's practices to explore further. The related Adventure Application appears just below each practice. If you'd prefer to come up with a different way of living out that practice this week, feel free to discuss what that might look like.

- *Be willing to step up and do a little more than usual when the situation requires it.*
  Marriage is not a fifty-fifty proposition. It requires a 100 percent commitment from each spouse. What can you do this week to begin to demonstrate that you understand and are committed to that in your marriage?

- *Seek to keep your romance alive, but be aware that it's normal for feelings to fluctuate and change over time; don't let unrealistic expectations of constant romance diminish your commitment to—or satisfaction with— your relationship.*
  This week, sit down with your spouse and discuss how your love for each other has changed and grown

stronger through the years. Take a few minutes to express gratitude to God and to each other.

- *Show the world that you are your partner's greatest fan.*
  Look for an opportunity to say something positive about your wife or husband this week, both privately and publicly. If you're tempted to criticize him or her, take a minute to weigh your words before you speak.

- *Care for the needs of your spouse's family as an expression of your love for your husband or wife.*
  Do you need to reach out to help someone in your spouse's family? Don't wait to be asked. Offer to do something for that family member and then make sure you follow through. Not only will you be loving as Christ commands us to be, but your spouse will be grateful and feel loved.

- *Build an uncommon marriage by staying focused on each other and allowing God to lead you.*
  As stress piles up, it can be more difficult to keep the focus off ourselves and our own problems. Take a few minutes to honestly consider where you are when it comes to turning your concerns over to God and leaning on your spouse for the support you need. Then bring any frustrations you feel to God in prayer.

- *Rest in the assurance that God, who promises never to leave or forsake you, knows what's ahead for your family.*
  What are you facing that you can't seem to see through or over or around into the next day? Remember that God hasn't gone anywhere; He will continue to fight for you as you wonder and stand ready to move ahead.

What can you do today to keep that truth in mind—and just stay calm?

UNCOMMON PRAYER

Take a few minutes to discuss any praises and needs you'd like to bring to God as a couple. Then, in addition to praying about those things, use one or more of the following prayer prompts to ask for God to deepen your love for and commitment to each other.

Praise God for designing you to enjoy intimacy with your spouse and for inviting you to enjoy that close relationship with Him as well.

Confess the times when your words or actions have not lifted up your spouse and perhaps have even cut him or her deeply.

Ask God to show you if there are ways you should be reaching out to another family member.

Thank God for walking with you through any trials you are currently facing.

day 71

LEARNING TO READ (EACH OTHER)

CORE PRACTICE #61:
Learn as much as you can about each other and how you each communicate before you get married.

....

My dove is hiding behind the rocks,
  behind an outcrop on the cliff.
Let me see your face;
  let me hear your voice.
For your voice is pleasant,
  and your face is lovely.

—SONG OF SONGS 2:14

Lauren

"Where should we go eat?"

   "Doesn't matter to me, as long as it's fairly quick."

   "Well . . . how about McDonald's?"

   "No, no fast food."

   "Well . . . how about Carrabba's?"

   "I don't feel like Italian tonight."

We've all been there, right? Tony tries to figure out what I'm saying—or not saying—and I'm doing the same, even after thirty-plus years! And it's not like either one of us is holding back intentionally; sometimes each of us gets stuck trying to figure out what *we* are trying to say.

Over the years, I've learned to be patient when Tony communicates. Or in his case, doesn't communicate. He's so much quieter than I am and is slower to express himself. As a result, I've learned to listen more and not react as emotionally.

That understanding didn't come overnight, though. When I'm slow to respond to Tony, it's likely because I disagree about something but want to communicate it to him nicely. So early in our marriage, when Tony hesitated before saying anything, I'd project my way of thinking on him and immediately conclude that he disagreed with me. Sometimes, that was the case. But more often, he was either searching for the right words or wanted to give something more thought before speaking.

I've also had to learn that even if Tony loves an idea, he may show that with only a small smile. I used to think, *Why isn't he more excited?* because he wasn't reacting with as much animation as I would. I've learned over time that's not a fair conclusion to reach—he just expresses his enthusiasm differently.

Don Meredith, a good friend of former Washington Redskins' head coach Joe Gibbs, talks about how such differences played out in his own marriage. In a chapter in Joe's book *Game Plan for Life*, Don describes the frustrations he and his wife, Sally, had early on. He was a hard-charging, goal-setting man. In contrast, Sally rolled with the situations God put before her.

Still, Don tried to explain to her the importance of goals and had her set daily and long-term goals. She felt uncomfortable trying to meet his expectations, and he was irritated by her response. How could she not see how helpful this practice was?

Then one day, the Lord showed Don that Sally's "weaknesses" weren't weaknesses. He finally understood that they were merely differences in the way his wife had been created. Her flexibility, Don realized, was a strength, especially when paired with his more rigid, linear personality. Together they were the perfect complement for each other, but it wasn't until he stopped judging her and tried to understand her that he could accept her as she was.[10]

This may be true for you and your spouse as well. The differences that may have seemed so intriguing while you were dating are likely to become irritations until you learn to understand and appreciate them.

Adventure Application: This week, if your spouse communicates in a way that perplexes or irritates you (or doesn't communicate at all), remind yourself that it's unlikely he or she is trying to bother you. Then consider the possibility that he or she is simply wired to respond that way.

day 72
DECISION TIME

CORE PRACTICE #62:
Accept others' input when making decisions, but listen the most to God and to each other.

....

Show me the right path, O LORD;
  point out the road for me to follow.
Lead me by your truth and teach me,
  for you are the God who saves.
All day long I put my hope in you.

—PSALM 25:4-5

TONY

Quarterback Drew Brees made headlines when he led the New Orleans Saints to a Super Bowl victory in 2010. Coming less than five years after Hurricane Katrina decimated the region, the victory represented a major comeback for the city—not to mention Drew himself.

Drew had played well for the San Diego Chargers, where he had started his career, but he hit the market as a free agent in 2006 after the Chargers made an offer during contract negotiations that he deemed low—even though he was recovering from a severe shoulder injury that he'd sustained in the last game of the 2005 season.

Of the other thirty-one teams in the National Football League, only the Miami Dolphins and the New Orleans Saints were interested in him as their starting quarterback. Other teams preferred him as a backup, especially in light of his rehabilitation for his injury. After flying to Miami and New Orleans to meet with both clubs, Drew and his wife, Brittany, sat down to recap their whirlwind tour.

The smart choice seemed to be Miami. New Orleans was still recovering from the devastation of Katrina, and the Dolphins had been better—much better—as a team in 2005. They'd gone 9–7 and finished the season on a six-game winning streak. The Saints, in the meantime, had won only three games all year.

Even the Breeses had thought it likely that they'd prefer Miami. But the couple had been unexpectedly affected by their visit to New Orleans, as Drew explains in his book:

> We sat on the bed and just stared at each other. The revelation seemed to hit us at the same time. We couldn't quite explain it, but it was almost like New Orleans was calling to us. We prayed together that night as we do every night, and we asked God to continue to show us what direction we should go. . . .
>
> We couldn't ignore the irresistible feeling—a sense of spiritual calling, even—that God wanted us in New Orleans. . . .
>
> Where some people might look at the city and see disaster, we saw opportunity. . . . We saw the adversity as a chance to build something special from the ground up. . . . What if God wanted us in New Orleans for such a time as this?[11]

And so Drew and Brittany headed to New Orleans. Drew came back from his injury to lead the Saints to greater success than most people could have imagined. More important, the Breeses are where God wants them, where they are able to make a difference.

If they'd listened to conventional wisdom, Drew probably would have taken the position in Miami. However, he and

Brittany prayed for guidance and looked to each other first for their most important input.

The right decision isn't always as clear to us as it was to the Breeses, and it doesn't always look so obviously correct after the fact. However, we still need to trust the Lord and trust our partner for guidance. After all, no one knew Drew's heart better than Brittany, and vice versa. We know what makes our spouse tick, what moves them, and what will provide the most satisfaction and meaning.

Adventure Application: Are you facing a major decision? Take it to the Lord in prayer—together—and discuss it with each other. Ask the Lord to give you His peace and comfort in the process.

day 73
TAKE TIME TO CONNECT

CORE PRACTICE #63:
Find a way to talk daily about what is happening in each other's life.

....

Encourage each other and build each other up, just as you are
already doing. . . . And live peacefully with each other.

—1 THESSALONIANS 5:11, 13

Lauren

Dinnertime at the Harris household was lively. My dad worked in real estate, and he loved to tell stories over the kitchen table about his clients and the homes they'd looked at. He and my mom always encouraged us kids to talk about our days too.

For the first few years of our marriage, I longed for the same kind of discussions with Tony when he arrived home after putting in ten or eleven hours at the office.

"How was your day? What's going on with the Steelers?" I'd ask after greeting him with a kiss.

"Oh, not too much, not too much" was his typical response as he started flipping through that day's mail. I knew he wasn't the most talkative guy, so before long I learned to initiate conversations. I'd listen to talk radio and watch the six o'clock news to see what I could use to begin a conversation with Tony later. That also enabled me to ask more direct questions about his day, like, "I heard five players were cut today. Is that really true?"

He'd nod and keep reading the mail. No progress.

Finally, we discussed it and made headway. It turns out he wasn't taking my opening as a cue to start a conversation; instead, he was thinking, *Well, if you heard it on TV, we don't need to rehash it. That's old news.* Especially if it wasn't earth-shattering. *Those are just little details,* he'd think. *She wouldn't be interested in hearing any more about that.*

Once he realized that my need for conversation wasn't for more information but for connection, he was open to setting aside time simply to talk. Finding the right time, however, was more of a challenge than we expected. After all, I'm more of a night owl whereas Tony heads to bed as soon as he gets tired . . . and he would usually come home tired!

Because Tony is quiet by nature, he needed to decompress when he first got home. But after dinner we took a walk, which was our chance to share our hearts with each other. As we did, we felt more connected and satisfied with our relationship.

A recent study backs up our experience. According to Angela Hicks, an associate professor of psychology at Westminster College in Salt Lake City, couples who discuss recent positive events every night feel better the following day, and are more intimate and connected with their spouses.[12]

It certainly has worked for us. It hasn't always been easy to find time to connect, but it's been so worth it. Turns out the little details don't matter so much in themselves—but talking about them matters a great deal.

Adventure Application: Do you set aside time regularly to talk with your spouse about his or her day? If so, keep it up! If not, discuss what is keeping you from connecting daily. How might you work that into your schedule?

day 74
WHEN TWO ARE WISER THAN ONE

CORE PRACTICE #64:
Listen to and value your spouse's intuition.

....

The wise are known for their understanding,
and pleasant words are persuasive. . . .
From a wise mind comes wise speech;
the words of the wise are persuasive.

Timely advice is lovely,
like golden apples in a silver basket.

—PROVERBS 16:21, 23; 25:11

Lauren

Tony takes people at face value. He's probably more trusting than I am. I prefer to call myself more analytical and perceptive, but maybe at times my approach comes off as cynical. I'd prefer not to think of it that way. All in all, we're a pretty good match. When the two of us discuss our varying perceptions, we generally reach a good understanding.

I've noticed this is often the case when repairmen come to our house. They tend to fall into one of two camps. Most everyone gets excited to see that they will be at Tony Dungy's house, and they're starstruck. But one group does whatever it takes to make the repair and ensure everything is working well again, even if it means going beyond what they might ordinarily do. The thought seems to be, *I don't want to disappoint Tony Dungy.*

Sometimes, though, repairmen will offer a detailed explanation of all they have to do and give us an enormous estimate for the cost of parts and labor. Inevitably, my usually frugal husband will respond, "Whatever you say. You're the expert."

On one occasion, a repairman came to fix our washer. I was busy elsewhere in the house during most of the service call, but I walked into our laundry room as the man was telling Tony that the necessary repairs were so extensive—and expensive—that we'd be better off buying a new machine.

I could tell my husband was ready to agree to that proposal, so while the repairman continued talking, I hurried to the file box where we keep our warranties. Carrying the paperwork back in with me, I asked the repairman, "We've only owned this machine for fourteen months. Isn't it still under warranty? According to this, the repairs shouldn't cost us anything except the fee for a service call."

After glancing at the warranty, the man nodded. No new washer needed.

On the flip side, Tony's trust leads to better decisions than I might make on my own. When Tony finally decided to write *Quiet Strength*, I asked him if he was sure about working with the writer Nathan Whitaker.

"I like Nathan," I told Tony. "But he hasn't written a book, and you've got a bunch of accomplished writers willing to do it. Are you sure?"

Tony nodded. "He says he can do it. I think he's right." I deferred to his intuition, and sure enough, it worked out well.

When we understand the way our spouse discerns situations, we may see the world in two very different but equally valid ways. Sometimes we may need to trust his or her viewpoint completely; at other times, we will come out ahead if we consider both our perspectives before making a decision. I like to picture that best-case scenario as the "golden apples in a silver basket" described in the proverb above.

Husband and wife; gold and silver. In both cases, one can complement the other perfectly.

Adventure Application: Do you and your spouse sometimes disagree about the best course to take? Could it be that one of you is more trusting and the other person more skeptical? Or are there some other terms to describe the different ways you see the world? Take a few minutes to discuss your approach.

day 75
THE GIFT OF GRATITUDE

CORE PRACTICE #65:
Remember that complaining will always bring you down;
gratitude will lift you up.

See that no one pays back evil for evil, but always try to do good to each other and to all people. Always be joyful. Never stop praying. Be thankful in all circumstances, for this is God's will for you who belong to Christ Jesus. —1 THESSALONIANS 5:15-18

TONY

One year after two bombings on Boston's Boylston Street stunned the country and disrupted America's most prestigious long-distance race, Meb Keflezighi won the 2014 Boston Marathon, the first American man to win in thirty-one years. He'd vowed to run in honor of those who had died, whose names he'd written on his running bib. Seconds after crossing the finish line to shouts of "USA! USA!" and "Boston Strong!" his wife, Yordanos, pulled him into a bear hug so tight that Meb told her, "You're gonna make me fall!"

I met Meb and Yordanos in 2011, and they are a truly inspiring couple. Meb is one of our country's greatest marathoners of all time, and Yordanos has had a huge role in his success. In addition to taking Boston's title, Meb won a silver medal in the marathon at the 2004 Olympics and won the 2009 New York City Marathon. He took fourth at the 2012 Olympics in London—the first (and only) American finisher.

What most people don't realize, however, is how many injuries Meb has had to overcome. During the 2008 Olympic Trials, he sustained a serious stress fracture to his hip that required many months of intensive rehab. Not long before the 2013 Boston Marathon, he injured his calf when he landed wrong on his foot after jumping over a dog that lunged at him during a training run. Meb, who was born in war-torn Eritrea and settled in America with his family when he was a young boy, knows what it means to persevere. But his wife has been the key to his ability to press on, even when the odds for a comeback appeared doubtful.

Running professionally is a full-time job for Meb, who must balance daily training and conditioning with personal appearances and frequent travel. Yordanos gave up her career in financial management to care for their three daughters and manage their household. She is also Meb's biggest cheerleader—even when injuries sideline him from a major race or a corporate sponsor drops him.

As friend and fellow Olympic marathoner Ryan Hall says, "She makes it possible for Meb to be the first one in the gym and the last one to leave." One reason Meb handles his obligations as a professional athlete so well, says Ryan, is because he knows that "his family is doing well at home. Yordanos is an incredibly empowering person in his life."[13]

In other words, whether in good times or bad, Yordanos chooses gratitude over complaining. A few years ago, when a reporter from *Running Times* followed Meb on a training run, Yordanos was also there to cheer on her husband. Giving him a high five, Yordanos smiled and said, "Looking good. You're the best-looking 37-year-old out there!"[14]

We'd all be wise to emulate Meb and Yordanos. So much of life depends on our attitude, and marriage is no different. Whether our spouse is pursuing a dream, driving children around town to various activities, or simply trying to stay ahead of the next round of corporate layoffs, showing gratitude toward them can do a lot to strengthen our marriages.

After all, complaining and whining never moves us to a better place. To improve in life, we need to focus on where we want to be. Our energies and emphasis will move us in that direction. Gratitude keeps our spirits up and our outlook bright. We realize God is always in control and will guide us through each day, helping us to overcome any anxiety or problem.

We may not have spectators cheering us on like those who kept Meb charging forward at the Boston Marathon; however, the words and attitude we offer to our spouse definitely influence how well we run our own race.

Adventure Application: Imagine your life as a long-distance race. How well are you cheering each other on? Would you say that a spirit of gratitude or of complaint more often characterizes the way you approach your spouse?

day 76
FAMILY TALK

CORE PRACTICE #66:
Model regular communication through family meetings.

....

Two people are better off than one, for they can help each other succeed.
If one person falls, the other can reach out and help. But someone who
falls alone is in real trouble. Likewise, two people lying close together
can keep each other warm. But how can one be warm alone? A person
standing alone can be attacked and defeated, but two can stand back-
to-back and conquer. Three are even better, for a triple-braided cord is
not easily broken. —ECCLESIASTES 4:9-12

TONY

Our family moved to Minnesota when our two oldest kids were
in elementary school. One of the decisions Lauren and I made
during that time was to begin having regular family meetings.
These meetings weren't called because something had gone
wrong, and they didn't take the place of the individual time we
spent with each child. But they became a time of fellowship and
connection between all family members, as well as an expected
part of our family routine.

By encouraging Tiara and Jamie to tell us what was going
on in their lives, they were affirmed, and we were able to show
them that we considered their activities just as important as
ours.

Sometimes one of the kids had a question or wanted to discuss a topic. Our family meetings also gave Lauren and me a
chance to talk through issues and encourage the kids: "I loved
the creativity you showed in that science report" or "How can

we be sure you fit in piano practice several times this week?" We also talked about activities we might want to do or trips we'd want to take as a family, and everyone's input was welcome.

They were not formal affairs by any means. Often we simply had them around the dinner table. The key was that everyone had to be there.

Over time, we realized these meetings also provided the kids with practice for speaking and organizing their thoughts, though that wasn't the reason to meet. As a rule there were to be no judgments rendered on anything said. Nothing was to be criticized, condemned, or proclaimed as silly. If there was a problem, Lauren or I would deal with it later with that child in private.

When we moved to Tampa, these regular family meetings took on a new importance. Because of my position as the head football coach of the Buccaneers, we sometimes felt as if we were living in a fish bowl, and it was important that we helped our children remain united, balanced, and on board with what we were doing as a family. And it was more important than ever that we kept up with what was going on in their lives.

Perhaps you like the idea of gathering your family together but aren't thrilled at the idea of calling it a "meeting." That's okay—call it anything you like. However, Lauren and I can vouch for the value of getting together with your children to talk about family life. As today's Scripture points out, there's always value in reaching out to each other to offer help, warmth, and protection. The family meeting may be one way to get it on your agenda.

Adventure Application: Do you have regularly scheduled family meetings? If so, do you need to make any tweaks for them to be more effective? If not, talk about whether they might make sense for your family.

day 77

PRINCIPLE 6
COMMUNICATE WELL AND OFTEN.

UNCOMMON WISDOM

Everyone enjoys a fitting reply;
* it is wonderful to say the right thing at the right time! . . .*
The heart of the godly thinks carefully before speaking;
* the mouth of the wicked overflows with evil words.*

—PROVERBS 15:23, 28

UNCOMMON PRACTICE

Take a few moments to select one of this week's practices to explore further. The related Adventure Application appears just below each practice. If you'd prefer to come up with a different way of living out that practice this week, feel free to discuss what that might look like.

- *Learn as much as you can about each other and how you each communicate before you get married.*
  This week, if your spouse communicates in a way that perplexes or irritates you (or doesn't communicate at all), remind yourself that it's unlikely he or she is trying to bother you. Then consider the possibility that he or she is simply wired to respond that way.

- *Accept others' input when making decisions, but listen the most to God and to each other.*
  Are you facing a major decision? Take it to the Lord in prayer—together—and discuss it with each other. Ask the Lord to give you His peace and comfort in the process.

- *Find a way to talk daily about what is happening in each other's life.*
  Do you set aside time regularly to talk with your spouse about his or her day? If so, keep it up! If not, discuss what is keeping you from connecting daily. How might you work that into your schedule?

- *Listen to and value your spouse's intuition.*
  Do you and your spouse sometimes disagree about the best course to take? Could it be that one of you is more trusting and the other person more skeptical? Or are there some other terms to describe the different ways you see the world? Take a few minutes to discuss your approach.

- *Remember that complaining will always bring you down; gratitude will lift you up.*
  Imagine your life as a long-distance race. How well are you cheering each other on? Would you say that a spirit of gratitude or of complaint more often characterizes the way you approach your spouse?

- *Model regular communication through family meetings.*
  Do you have regularly scheduled family meetings? If so, do you need to make any tweaks for them to be more effective? If not, talk about whether they might make sense for your family.

UNCOMMON PRAYER

Take a few minutes to discuss any praises and needs you'd like to bring to God as a couple. Then, in addition to praying about those things, use one or more of the following prayer prompts to ask the Lord to help you communicate with each other more regularly, lovingly, and clearly.

Praise God for one or more of His many attributes, remembering that only when we get our focus off ourselves and on to Him will we find reasons to be grateful in all circumstances.

If you found yourself grumbling or complaining this week, confess that to God. Ask Him to give you a heart that overflows with gratitude this week.

Seek the Lord's guidance as you consider any decisions this week. Ask that He would give you peace and a sense of harmony as you move ahead.

day 78
TWO-WAY CONVERSATION

CORE PRACTICE #67:
Pay attention to and use your spouse's preferred form of communication.

....

Don't use foul or abusive language. Let everything you say be good and helpful, so that your words will be an encouragement to those who hear them. Get rid of all bitterness, rage, anger, harsh words, and slander, as well as all types of evil behavior. Instead, be kind to each other, tenderhearted, forgiving one another, just as God through Christ has forgiven you. —EPHESIANS 4:29, 31-32

Lauren

I mentioned earlier how much Tony and I have learned from Gary Chapman's book *The 5 Love Languages*. Chapman says that if couples are to maintain the level of emotional love they felt when they first married, they must understand and use their spouse's primary love language. Each of us has a love language that, when "spoken" by our spouse, makes us feel loved. These languages are words of affirmation; quality time; receiving gifts; acts of service; and physical touch.[15]

I think these love languages are also related to the way we like to connect with other people. In the early years of our marriage, Tony would watch me as I talked on the phone with my mom for long periods of time. Tony saw that I was a relational person who felt affirmed when I was able to talk with other people. That's why, when we moved because of his job change, I tried to build friendships as soon as possible, both in the neighborhood and in a new church.

But I also wanted to hear from Tony. And so he would always

try to call me, in between meetings and practices, even if we could talk for only a few minutes. He also knew that spending time with him was important to me, so we did our best to carve out time for regular evening walks together.

It worked both ways. I needed to take even the smallest opportunity to express my appreciation for Tony and what he did for me and the children. That, I had quickly discovered, was very affirming to him. Because of that, I intentionally sought out those moments when I could encourage him.

What's important to me or to Tony might not resonate with you. That's okay. We all have different preferences when it comes to communicating and listening to each other. We're different in what makes us feel affirmed, respected, and loved. You may feel cared for when your spouse gives you a word of support; you might prefer that he or she simply listen without speaking or trying to fix things.

As we grow under God's protective and guiding hand, it's important to remember that He created each of us as unique individuals, but He also brought us together. No matter what we face, we can find a pathway to resolution and peace if we seek to honor each other—and maybe even ask our Creator to show us the love language He's hardwired into our spouse.

Adventure Application: If you and your spouse have identified your love language, talk for a few minutes about how it affects the way you like to communicate with others. If you've never given your love languages much thought, you might visit http://www.5lovelanguages.com/, which provides much more information.

day 79
OF ONE MIND

CORE PRACTICE #68:
Ask whether you both have peace and are on the same page before committing to a major decision.

Don't worry about anything; instead, pray about everything. Tell God what you need, and thank him for all he has done. Then you will experience God's peace, which exceeds anything we can understand. His peace will guard your hearts and minds as you live in Christ Jesus. —PHILIPPIANS 4:6-7

Lauren

I think Tony first knew something was up when I told him, "Boy, this house is really quiet."

We had moved to Tampa a few years before, and now that we were settled and our three kids were in school all day, I felt God beginning to speak to me as I asked Him what His plans were for us. Not only had I always wanted a large family, but because Tony and I had been foster parents and my own mom and dad had adopted two children late in life, I sensed God nudging me to explore that option.

When I pray and God tugs at my heart about something He wants me to do, I know I need to be obedient. I was ready to begin exploring adoption. Yet I knew this decision wasn't mine alone to make.

While I believe sacrifice and compromise are sometimes called for from both partners, we need to move with caution when asking our spouse to consider a "major" change. Adoption is one such issue. While adding a child to the family always brings joy, it also may require great commitment and sacrifice.

When I first discussed adoption, Tony was hesitant because of his age. He wondered whether it was the right time. We talked a great deal about that, and he was open to my getting more information. Just as I had been supportive of his passion for football, he wanted to hear my heart on adoption. Both of us knew, however, that this wasn't an area for compromise. We weren't going to weigh how strongly I was for it versus how strongly Tony was against it. If Tony wasn't on board, we wouldn't proceed.

In fact, Tony and I tell couples it's never wise to adopt if both spouses aren't behind that decision. Likewise, decisions such as whether to move cross country, start a new business, or add on to your house need to be carefully discussed by both spouses. If you aren't on the same page, consider that a warning sign to proceed with caution before moving ahead. There's almost always more time to reach a mutual decision; it's usually much harder to undo one.

After I'd done some research on adoption and we'd discussed how we felt about moving ahead, Tony and I agreed it was worth meeting with a caseworker. After I'd asked a number of questions, she looked at Tony and said, "Mr. Dungy, you've been awfully quiet. Do you have anything you'd like to ask?"

Tony said, "I have just one question. If we decide to do this, how long is this going to take?"

"If you're interested in an African American or biracial child," she said, "you could take a child home in a month."

That answer stunned Tony, who had just watched as one of the Bucs' assistant coaches welcomed his adopted son after more than a yearlong process. When Tony heard that we could have a child that quickly, he took it as God's confirmation that our family—with more than enough love and resources to go around—should adopt a child. It wasn't enough to call ourselves pro-life and encourage women not to have abortions. We had to step up and honor the decision of a woman in that situation.

Not long after, one-day-old Jordan joined our family. Since our next youngest child, Eric, was nine at the time, I soon told Tony I wanted to adopt one more baby so Jordan wouldn't grow up feeling like an only child.

But since that time, we have adopted five more children. "I should have known it wasn't going to be just one more," Tony likes to joke.

Adventure Application: How satisfied are you with your process for making major decisions? Do you both feel valued and included? Are there any decisions that you should discuss even now?

day 80
"DO WHAT I SAY . . . AND WHAT I DO"

CORE PRACTICE #69:
Remember that, with your words, you are teaching your kids how to speak to others.

....

Direct your children onto the right path,
 and when they are older, they will not leave it.

—PROVERBS 22:6

TONY

Our children are watching, whether we like it or not. I was reminded of that again several years ago, when our son Jordan was seven years old.

By then, he'd become familiar with my typical reaction whenever something goes wrong—whether on the football field or at home. Almost always, the first words out of my mouth are "You've *got* to be kidding me!"

So when his two-year-old brother, Justin, broke one of his favorite toys, Jordan's first response was, "You've *got* to be kidding me!" (He even put just the right emphasis on the word *got.*)

You're not surprised, are you? Kids are little sponges. They soak up whatever preferences or behaviors they are exposed to at home, whether it's a love for books, sports, or the use of particular phrases.

We need to be careful about what we allow to come out of our mouths when we are around our children—especially when we are tired. That means guarding our thinking too. As Paul reminds us, we should "fix [our] thoughts on what is true, and . . . excellent" (Philippians 4:8).

Filling our minds with the good, the pure, and the true things of life seems like a good practice, but it isn't always easy. It can be a particular challenge when we're being served by a waiter, a salesclerk, or a cab driver. It can be easy to fall into the mind-set that because we're paying for the service, we should be able to treat the provider in whatever manner we choose.

However, I want to show my children the importance of recognizing each person as a child of God. Therefore, as my children watch me place an order with a waiter, approach a clerk with a question, or give an address to a cab driver, I pray they see how I would like them to speak to others in any circumstance.

I have learned a lot about this from my friend James Brown. James is a sportscaster for CBS, and we often stay at the same hotel in New York during the football season. He is one of the nicest people I know and has never met a stranger. I've seen him interact with everyone from bellhops and custodians to broadcasters and Supreme Court justices. JB shares our mind-set that everybody matters, and he lives it out. He takes time with every person and gives grace to whomever he is speaking . . . you'd never know who they were. But I think it says even more about JB, and I hope I model the same courtesy and respect.

Adventure Application: Do either you or your spouse use any "catchphrases" that you've noticed your children picking up on? If so, and that's a pattern you don't want to encourage, how can you help each other replace those words with more positive expressions?

day 81
TECH TALK

CORE PRACTICE #70:
Use technology to keep you connected; don't allow it to pull you apart.

....

For everything there is a season,
* a time for every activity under heaven. . . .*
A time to search and a time to quit searching.
* A time to keep and a time to throw away.*

—ECCLESIASTES 3:1, 6

Lauren

Tony and I made appearances throughout Indiana while we were with the Colts. One interesting aspect of traveling the state's highways was seeing members of the Amish community.

I was under the impression that the Amish shunned all technology, preferring to maintain their traditions and values. Instead, I've learned that they analyze technology with an eye toward what influence, if any, it will have on those traditions and values. If the impact is positive, they will adopt the new technology completely or modify it if necessary. If they believe the impact would be negative, they simply won't allow it to come into their community. That's why they shun the use of all mass media technology, such as televisions, radios, and personal computers.

We have a different approach to modern technology, but there is great wisdom in the Amish philosophy. Before allowing a new technology into our home, we ask ourselves if it will be good for our family. If there are downsides, we discuss the limits we should put in place.

Our son Jordan is a genius with electronics. Thank goodness!

He doesn't have to read the instructions to know how to operate most gadgets. He programs all of our remote controls, sets up all of our family's computers, and troubleshoots them whenever something isn't working.

Some of that technology has been great. Jordan taught us how to Skype with his two oldest siblings, an amazing advance that has allowed our family to shrink the geographical distance between us and keep us connected.

But as the writer of Ecclesiastes says, there is a time and a season for everything, and the Amish appreciate this attitude. The Internet, which allows us to Skype, also contains destructive forces that we don't want to bring into our home, so we've placed limits on our devices.

In addition, we've set parameters on when those devices can be used. For example, we don't allow Jordan to bring any electronics to the dinner table, and he can't turn anything on until he's finished his homework. Plus, we have time limits so that Jordan doesn't become consumed with electronics—after all, we want some direct face time with him too.

To me, it's a balancing act. Skype, e-mail, and mobile phones can link us with our family and friends in ways we couldn't have imagined even a few decades ago. Paradoxically, if we're not vigilant, those same technologies can isolate us.

At the end of the day, the best way to stay connected is to be with others. If there's a way for the latest device to help with that, terrific. But not at the expense of it taking away from the time that we spend making memories together.

Adventure Application: Whenever the latest and greatest device, program, or app comes along, decide what kind of influence it could have on your family. When it comes to technology, is there anything you should revisit? Phones during meals? Certain time constraints for video games or movies? Limits on the Internet?

day 82
HONORING OTHERS WITH YOUR WORDS

CORE PRACTICE #71:
Seek to honor your spouse and children by the way you speak about them to others.

Reward her for all she has done.
    Let her deeds publicly declare her praise.

—PROVERBS 31:31

TONY

Earlier, I told you about the Colts' incredible victory over the Bucs in October 2003. While that matchup had incredible personal meaning for me, the media also followed the pregame preparations closely, and a number of them called for interviews, asking how it felt to be going up against our former team.

Lauren and I had been looking forward to the contest, although after hearing over and over that everyone thought the Colts were going to get creamed, we wondered what type of reception we'd receive on game day.

But Lauren wasn't going to let that negativity keep her from being there to support me. If anything, it made her more resolved to be there. So she and Tiara, wearing their Colts gear, met a group of friends before the game. Almost from the time they arrived, they were booed; they even got pelted with Cokes as they made their way to their seats. If that wasn't enough, the Bucs controlled the scoreboard during the first two quarters. It was 21–0 at halftime. Except for cheering on the Colts, Lauren held her tongue—even when some Bucs fans suggested she head back to Indiana's cornfields (never mind that she was living with the kids in Tampa).

We played better in the second half, but with five minutes to go, we still trailed 35–14. The Bucs fans were now too busy celebrating to bother Lauren and Tiara. But the unbelievable was about to happen. After scoring three consecutive touchdowns and then kicking a field goal in overtime to win, it was now our turn to celebrate.

It was one of my most satisfying victories, but I knew that win or lose, Lauren would be waiting for me, as always, outside the locker room. This time, she also presented me with a huge birthday cake—decked out in the Colts' colors—to share with the team after the game.

Lauren has always been consistent about speaking well of me, both by her actions and by what she says when I've been questioned by frustrated fans or media.

We all know the importance of our words. And while it's true that we can hurt anyone by our careless words, how much deeper does the wound go when we inflict it on the person who loves us most?

What we say really does matter. A lot.

God created the family structure as a place of safety and a place where husbands and wives can model what it means to love each other unconditionally. Is your home a sanctuary? Are your family members safe there? Not just physically, but in what they hear?

So often a stray word directed to a spouse or a child remains with them indefinitely. And what we say about family members in public can damage their reputations. That's why making hasty comments to people outside our family—even when we think those words will never get back to our family members— can be so destructive.

Sometimes, as Lauren demonstrated, it's best to say nothing

at all to our spouse's critics and instead to offer words of affirmation and support for our husband or wife. That often says more than any clever comeback ever could.

Adventure Application: Do you build up your spouse and children when you discuss them with others? Would you be comfortable if they heard what you were saying? What about when you speak to them? Are you giving them your blessing? If not, think about your words and how you might use them as a tool for good.

day 83
CREATING A GODLY BLUEPRINT

CORE PRACTICE #72:
Remember that the way you are relating to each other is creating a blueprint for your kids.

I will teach you hidden lessons from our past—stories we have heard and known, stories our ancestors handed down to us. We will not hide these truths from our children; we will tell the next generation about the glorious deeds of the LORD, about his power and his mighty wonders. —PSALM 78:2-4

Lauren

When I was young, my parents planned their dream home. I still remember them sitting down every evening to discuss each aspect of the home—the location, the style, the features. My dad, being in real estate, knew the best place to build and what the size of the lot should be. My mom had more expertise when it came to the features of the home—its design, style, and layout.

As they talked, one thing became clear: It wasn't her house, nor was it his house. It was theirs. They worked together, and they pored over the plans and talked about them every day for months. During that time, they heard each other's wish list. We all knew that our new home was a joint project.

Looking back, I realize they were developing another set of blueprints at the same time. By communicating openly and with respect, they were showing me and my siblings how a married couple should relate to each other. Tony's parents were doing the same for him and his brothers and sister. Much of who Tony and I are today was shaped by how we saw our parents talk to each other, deal with each other, and handle disagreements.

My mom is a strong-minded woman of faith. She's a godly, Proverbs 31 woman. Tony says that I am very much like her. By contrast, Tony is very analytical—just like his father was. Whenever something comes up that Tony isn't sure how to handle, he still figures out a way to get it done . . . after carefully mapping the course. Watching his dad triumph over challenges has guided Tony so many times over the years.

We are now working to do for our children what our parents did for us—create a godly blueprint of how to relate to others. The blueprint does more than give them an example of how to treat their spouse one day. It shows them how to treat everyone they meet today. It also provides a sense of security for our children. They feel safe because the people they count on the most love each other and will always be there for them.

Just as our parents were for us.

Adventure Application: What "blueprint" are you leaving for your children? If you've never thought about this before, you might spend a few minutes brainstorming the qualities you'd like others to see as they watch you interact. What is one change you can make this week to provide a better model of positive communication?

day 84

PRINCIPLE 6
COMMUNICATE WELL AND OFTEN.

UNCOMMON WISDOM

Walk with the wise and become wise;
  associate with fools and get in trouble.

—PROVERBS 13:20

UNCOMMON PRACTICE

Take a few moments to select one of this week's practices to explore further. The related Adventure Application appears just below each practice. If you'd prefer to come up with a different way of living out that practice this week, feel free to discuss what that might look like.

- *Pay attention to and use your spouse's preferred form of communication.*
  If you and your spouse have identified your love language, talk for a few minutes about how it affects the way you like to communicate with others. If you've never given your love languages much thought, you might visit http://www.5lovelanguages.com/, which provides much more information.

- *Ask whether you both have peace and are on the same page before committing to a major decision.*
  How satisfied are you with your process for making major decisions? Do you both feel valued and included?

Are there any decisions that you should discuss even now?

- *Remember that, with your words, you are teaching your kids how to speak to others.*
  Do either you or your spouse use any "catchphrases" that you've noticed your children picking up on? If so, and if that's a pattern you don't want to encourage, how you can help each other replace those words with more positive expressions?

- *Use technology to keep you connected; don't allow it to pull you apart.*
  Whenever the latest and greatest device, program, or app comes along, take the time to decide if its influence on your family will be positive or negative. When it comes to technology, is there anything you should revisit? Phones during meals? Certain time constraints for video games or movies? Limits on the Internet?

- *Seek to honor your spouse and children by the way you speak about them to others.*
  Do you build up your spouse and children when you discuss them with others? Would you be comfortable if they heard what you were saying? What about when you speak to them? Are you giving them your blessing? If not, think about your words and how you might use them as a tool for good.

- *Remember that the way you are relating to each other is creating a blueprint for your kids.*
  What "blueprint," or plan, do you have for speaking the best of each other for the sake of your kids and

others who are watching you? If you've never thought about this before, you might spend a few minutes brainstorming the qualities you'd like others to see as they watch you interact. What is one change you can make this week to provide a better model of positive communication?

UNCOMMON PRAYER

Take a few minutes to discuss any praises and needs you'd like to bring to God as a couple. Then, in addition to praying about those things, use one or more of the following prayer prompts to ask the Lord to help you communicate with each other more regularly, lovingly, and clearly.

Praise God for communicating His love and acceptance of you so clearly through Scripture, Jesus' death and resurrection, and the Holy Spirit's work in your lives.

Confess any instances this week when your communication— whether through words, body language, or even silence—made another person feel rejected, condemned, or discouraged.

Ask the Holy Spirit to give you wisdom as you discuss limits to place on the use of technology—particularly by your children.

Lift up each member of your household by name, thanking God for his or her presence in your lives and asking Him to help you encourage and challenge that person to become a man or woman after God's own heart.

day 85
WEIGHING YOUR WORDS

CORE PRACTICE #73:
Watch what you say—even the truth can wound when it's spoken in the wrong way or at the wrong time.

A gentle answer deflects anger,
but harsh words make tempers flare.
The tongue of the wise makes knowledge appealing,
but the mouth of a fool belches out foolishness.

—PROVERBS 15:1-2

TONY

A number of pastors and their wives attended a three-day retreat. During one session, they were invited to tell a story about how God was working in their lives and ministries. One young woman stood up nervously. She said, "The Bible promises, 'No good thing will [the Lord] withhold from them that walk uprightly.' Well," she said with great feeling, "my husband is one of those 'no good things'!"[16]

All of us misspeak at times. I can't tell you how many times I have said something and wished I could reach out, grab the words, and stuff them back into my mouth before they reached Lauren's ears. I fight the tendency to allow my tongue to have its own way. As the apostle James reminds us:

> The tongue is a flame of fire. It is a whole world of wickedness . . . Sometimes it praises our Lord and Father, and sometimes it curses those who have been made in the image of God. And so blessing and

cursing come pouring out of the same mouth. Surely,
my brothers and sisters, this is not right! (3:6, 9-10)

It may seem fairly inconsequential to tell someone "That's
stupid," or "That's the dumbest thing I have ever heard you say."
But even when those words aren't spoken in anger, they tend
to hurt and wound. And when they are directed toward your
spouse—well, they hurt even more.

Sometimes we make the situation worse by trying to mini-
mize the damage. How many times have you found yourself
saying, "That's not what I meant," "You misunderstood," or
"I'm sorry that's how it came across"? I know I do that too often.

Of course, a cutting remark tends to elicit a sharp answer.
When something is said to me that rubs me the wrong way,
I have to fight the impulse to strike back. The apostle Paul
encourages you and me to "let your conversation be gracious and
attractive so that you will have the right response for everyone"
(Colossians 4:6). In this section of his letter, Paul is telling the
Colossians how to live the new life they have received in Christ.
Knowing how impossible it is to live this way—and to speak
graciously—in our own strength, he adds, "Remember the Lord
forgave you, so you must forgive others. Above all, clothe yourselves with love" (Colossians 3:13-14). In other words, speaking
graciously may not be as easy as it first appears!

Of course, weighing our words before speaking doesn't mean
we never have difficult conversations with each other. In all
things and at all times, we need to share the truth. But according to the apostle Paul, it's when we "speak the truth in love"
that we grow "more and more like Christ" (Ephesians 4:15).
That means taking care not to wound unnecessarily with our
words. Sometimes we may need to wait—to leave something
unsaid—until our anger has cooled and we can measure our

thoughts. At other times, it's best to allow someone else, whose words will be better received than ours, to speak candidly.

Talk may be cheap, but it can exact a high price. By choosing our words carefully and delivering them in a caring tone of voice, we will help make our home the most uplifting and safest place in the world for our family.

Adventure Application: What words have you said to your spouse this week that you wish you could take back? Why not run them by your husband or wife, asking for forgiveness if necessary?

day 86
OPEN ADMISSION

CORE PRACTICE #74:
Avoid frustration and seek to understand each other's heart by praying together and talking with each other.

Understand this, my dear brothers and sisters: You must all be quick to listen, slow to speak, and slow to get angry. —JAMES 1:19

Lauren

Ken met his future wife at church. With her blonde hair and wide smile, she was a beautiful woman, inside and out. Everyone who met her adored her. An accomplished author and speaker, she had traveled the world. Ken enjoyed talking with her, and soon he asked her out on a date. Within a year, the couple had married. It sounds like the ideal love story, right? So why had so many of his friends wondered why he was attracted to her?

Fifteen years before their wedding, Ken's wife, Joni, had become a quadriplegic after a diving accident. The first months and years that followed were excruciating for her. By the time she and Ken met, however, both were in their early thirties and had successful careers. Ken was a high school teacher and coach; Joni was a bestselling author, painter, and the founder of Joni and Friends, a ministry dedicated to others with disabilities.

Despite their deep love for each other, Ken began to wear out just a few years after they married. In addition to helping Joni with day-to-day needs, like dressing and putting on makeup, he taught all day and did all their shopping in the evenings.

Eventually, Ken told Joni he felt trapped and worn out. But, he added, he also felt guilty for feeling that way.

"If I were you," Joni told him, "I'd feel exactly the same way."[17]

As difficult as that conversation was, it appears to have freed them to be more open with each other. They refused to look at each other as the enemy; instead, they sought more outside help and made it a point to affirm the other. To remain centered, they read the Bible and prayed together.

So often, frustration mounts between a couple because they fear each other's reaction to their struggles and doubts. Yet those who build strong marriages aren't afraid to admit these difficulties; they do, however, avoid using them to hurt or take advantage of their spouse. They see themselves as allies who want the best for their marriage and aren't afraid of the hard work needed to build a lasting relationship. They make time to speak and to listen to each other. And rather than bury conflict, they bring it into the light and hash it out.

When I read the story of the Tadas' marriage recently, I noticed a couple of similarities to our own. Like us, Joni and Ken married in the summer of 1982. They frequently speak and minister together. And, like me, Joni encouraged her husband to pursue his interest in fishing (though Ken prefers fly-fishing; Tony, saltwater fishing). As you now know, the Tadas also value open and honest communication—and that may be the most important similarity of all.

Adventure Application: On a scale of 1 to 10, how safe would each of you say you feel with the other? It's okay to admit that you've drifted far apart; in fact, when two people who care for each other confess their fears or lament the distance between them, they've taken the first step to a closer relationship. If you don't feel safe—physically or emotionally—with your spouse, it's time to seek help from an outside counselor.

day 87

A HOUSE DIVIDED

CORE PRACTICE #75:
Practice thinking about an issue on which you disagree from your spouse's point of view.

....

They must not slander anyone and must avoid quarreling. Instead, they should be gentle and show true humility to everyone. —TITUS 3:2

TONY

You've probably heard about the volatile relationship between our sixteenth president, Abraham Lincoln, and his wife, Mary Todd. In fact, their differences were stark: He was a backwoods lawyer and politician; she, a refined Southern aristocrat. Both were ambitious, though Mary seemed to have factored that aspiration into her decision to marry the tall, gangly lawyer. About four years after their marriage, Abraham introduced her to a colleague during a party at their house. After greeting the man, Mary said about her husband, "He is to be President of the United States some day; if I had not thought so I never would have married him, for you can see he is not pretty."[18] Before you're too hard on Mary, consider what Abraham told the wife of a friend about eighteen months before they wed: "It would just kill me to marry Mary Todd."[19]

Their relationship remained unsettled after their marriage. When they got into an argument, Mary would sometimes scream and throw things. Most often, her husband just walked away. (No doubt he was grateful that, as a circuit-riding lawyer, he had to travel to try cases about six months out of the year.) In their years together, Mary soothed herself by shopping and then tried to keep her purchases secret from her frugal husband. In one three-month period, she bought three hundred pairs of gloves.

Interestingly, there is evidence that Abraham was proud of his wife and that Mary Todd idolized her husband. Yet it seems they never mastered the art of considering things from the other's perspective. Nor did either learn how to converse effectively. Abraham apparently said little at home, and Mary spoke quite a lot but said little to build up her husband or their marriage. Sadly, they appear to have lived in a house divided.

While I'm not sure it would have helped the Lincolns, I like the word picture that Erwin Lutzer, pastor of Chicago's Moody Church, provides to help other spouses in unhappy marriages consider the source of their frustration. "Put a pencil in a glass of water and it will appear crooked. In the same way, our perceptions of others, and especially our perception of ourselves, is always skewed. . . . Anger, pride, and selfishness cause us to see everyone else (particularly our marriage partner) as bent."[20]

According to the apostle Paul, the antidote to having a distorted view of someone else is to be gentle and humble in our approach to that person. In a marriage, that means acknowledging and accepting our spouse's unique makeup—even when we're as different as the humble Abe Lincoln and his aristocratic wife.

Adventure Application: As you go about your daily tasks at home, do you find that you get irritated over the same type of issues with your spouse? If so, talk about what may drive your differences in those areas.

day 88
THE ENEMIES WITHIN

CORE PRACTICE #76:
Don't assume your spouse understands how you feel—particularly when life gets busy.

....

Hatred stirs up quarrels,
but love makes up for all offenses.
—PROVERBS 10:12

TONY

Because people in our culture usually marry for love, it's a bit jarring to consider how infrequently we read of a person in the Bible expressing romantic feelings for someone else.

Of course we know that Jacob ended up working fourteen years so he could marry the love of his life, Rachel. And Song of Songs celebrates romance between a man and woman. Yet only once does a writer directly mention a woman's growing infatuation toward a man: "Saul's daughter Michal had fallen in love with David" (1 Samuel 18:20). To us, that declaration may not be surprising, but in her day, princesses like Michal were married off by their fathers—and we can be sure that both Saul and any potential suitors would be looking to make a match that would benefit them personally.

In this case, King Saul offered Michal to David only because it gave him an opportunity to bait the younger man into battle against the Philistines—who Saul hoped would kill David. David's motives weren't pure either. There's no hint he loved Michal; however, marrying the king's daughter would raise his status considerably.

Yet it appears Michal was deeply committed to her new husband. No modern-day romance novel or movie better portrays the lengths a woman will go to protect the man she loves than the story we read in 1 Samuel 19. When Saul was determined to assassinate David, Michal helped him escape. Only because she convinced her father that David would have killed her if she hadn't helped him get away did Saul spare his daughter's life.

Unfortunately, that is the final loving interaction we see between David and Michal. The young warrior took refuge in the wilderness, and it would be years before he saw his bride again. In the meantime, he took two additional wives, and Saul eventually married Michal off again, this time to a man named Palti, son of Laish, who clearly adored her.[21]

After Saul was killed in battle, David finally sent for Michal, even though that meant tearing her away from her new husband. It's unlikely David was motivated by love, but getting her back would strengthen his claim to her father's throne. Any affection between the couple had evaporated by the time David returned to Jerusalem with the Ark of the Covenant, celebrating with exuberance as he went. Michal, a proper princess, berated him for dancing with such abandon before the Lord; in response, David dismissed her remarks. He even seemed to take a jab at her family, noting that God "chose me above your father and all his family!" (2 Samuel 6:21).

This strange love story obviously had taken a very dark turn. Without knowing more details, it's hard to know where to assign blame. Multiple outside forces had certainly conspired against their marriage too. However, both David and Michal both carry some responsibility for the implosion of their marriage since one or both were guilty at times of neglect, disdain, jealousy, and disrespect.

Fortunately, in our day, we aren't threatened by political feuds or the threat of banishment; however, we must guard against an enemy unique to our time and culture: busyness. When we're so consumed with other priorities, we may ignore our spouse just as certainly as David seems to have overlooked Michal.

So today, commit to making each other a high priority, recognizing that while your feelings and circumstances may change, your commitment should not.

Adventure Application: Whether you'd rate your marriage as strong or struggling, you and your spouse need to be on guard against anything that might get between you. Take a few minutes to discuss whether factors like busyness, hurt feelings, or misunderstandings are creating barriers between you. If so, begin talking through them. And don't be afraid to ask a wise Christian couple or counselor for help.

day 89
HONESTY ~~IS~~ CAN BE A VIRTUE

CORE PRACTICE #77:
Be bold and speak the truth in love.

....

We will speak the truth in love, growing in every way more and more like Christ, who is the head of his body, the church. —EPHESIANS 4:15

Lauren

"Really, James? Why don't you listen? I've told you not to put my jeans in the dryer—now they're too tight!"

"Maybe if you'd eat more salads and less junk food, Cathy, or make use of your gym membership, it wouldn't matter if I forgot."

Honest? Sure. Speaking your mind? Sounds like James and Cathy are definitely speaking their minds—without a filter.

Honesty is certainly a trait to value. In fact, it's a major component of the foundation of a fulfilling marriage, one that's based on trust and openness, not deception and secrets. A major building block, to be sure.

Plus, a healthy marriage is not one in which the partners feel they must suppress their feelings and opinions. Tony and I have tried to create an environment of transparency and honesty by expressing our needs, feelings, thoughts, and hurts to each other.

But we cannot treat the command for honesty and intimacy as a license to say anything we want. Before blurting out what first comes to our minds, I think we need to ask ourselves: *Would I use that tone with a friend?* If we think, *Of course not,* why, then, would we use it with our spouse?

When we speak to a close friend, it's no less important that we speak with transparency and boldness, but I daresay that you—like me—would find a way to cautiously lead into a difficult conversation and couch your remarks in a way intended to cause minimal offense. So why would we take a shortcut when it comes to communicating with our spouse?

In her book *The Surprising Secrets of Highly Happy Marriages*, Shaunti Feldhahn writes that happily married couples don't communicate using brutal honesty. In the chapter "Don't Tell It Like It Is," Shaunti notes that, instead, happily married couples focus on being *kindly* honest, sprinkling gentleness into the conversation, and never becoming disrespectful.[22]

That's an important point. Being bold and honest does not mean being cruel, heartless, or insensitive. It doesn't mean removing the filter that keeps us from saying something hurtful or destructive.

One key to dealing constructively with conflict is to avoid letting it build. That's yet another reason to make a point to talk daily about what's on your hearts and minds. If you communicate regularly, you will catch issues early. When you don't suppress feelings for a long time, you avoid the danger that they might unexpectedly erupt—which usually doesn't end well. Working through differences calmly, with a commitment not to tease or otherwise belittle each other, makes a huge difference in resolving conflict well.

And that's always better than airing your dirty laundry, as James and Cathy did!

Adventure Application: Think about your communication pattern. Is it healthy? Are you able to be honest with each other without being destructive? Stay honest, but commit to remove sarcasm, disrespect, and other forms of "brutal honesty" from your conversations with your spouse.

day 90
DOING THE IMPOSSIBLE

CORE PRACTICE #78: Expect that when your emotions and perceptions don't line up, conflict will occur.

....

I know how to live on almost nothing or with everything. I have learned the secret of living in every situation, whether it is with a full stomach or empty, with plenty or little. For I can do everything through Christ, who gives me strength. —PHILIPPIANS 4:12-13

TONY

After being stabbed by another sharp rebuttal or enduring another night of stony silence, have you ever told yourself, *I can't do this! My spouse just doesn't understand me, and marriage is so much harder than I ever imagined*?

If so, I have good news and bad news. I'll give you the bad news first: You're right. You *can't* do it—not on your own. You and your spouse are two flawed human beings whose different failings, feelings, and perceptions will often lead you to clash. When you add fatigue, illness, or other stressors (such as children) to the mix, that conflict may seem insurmountable.

But I can guarantee this: The good news trumps the bad.

Christ promises you all the grace and strength you need. When Paul wrote to the church in Philippi, he was addressing believers who were being marginalized and brutalized because they had decided to follow God. Paul himself was in prison, so he knew the pressure of trying to stand strong in a difficult situation. Pastor Tony Evans says this about today's Scripture passage: "[Paul] wasn't saying that he could fly on his own power if he chose to, but he was promising that everything

Christ commanded him to do, Christ would enable him to accomplish."[23]

Did you catch that? Since God commanded us to love and respect our spouses, He will give us the power to do it—provided we look to Him and follow where He leads.

Likewise the author of Hebrews urges us to "run with endurance the race God has set before us. We do this by keeping our eyes on Jesus, the champion who initiates and perfects our faith" (Hebrews 12:1-2). In other words, we are to look to Him.

I know Lauren and I have mentioned several times that we pray together every day. Now do you see why? We know our shortcomings; we know our limitations; we know we are unaware of much that lies ahead of us. And when we feel locked in a bad situation with no way out, we know where our only source of hope and understanding is found.

"Conflicts shouldn't destroy the union," says Evans, "they should show the power of Christ within us. Because Christ never asks us to do what He has not already given us the ability to do, marital conflict can be the area in which we show the difference Christ makes."[24]

Amazing, isn't it? Not only does God promise to walk with us through any troubles with our spouse, He can use our struggles to show the world that He is faithful, loving, and all-powerful.

Before giving up, be sure to look up. Today, if you feel stuck in a deep pit of despair, maybe these insights from pastor John Piper will provide just the hope you need: "With God, nothing is impossible. He has more ropes and ladders and tunnels out of pits than you can conceive. Wait. Pray without ceasing. Hope."[25]

Adventure Application: Where are you looking? Down in defeat? At each other with eyes blazing? Or up to the one who promises that you can do anything through Him? If you're not already looking up, how can you help each other do that?

PRINCIPLE 7
DON'T RUN AWAY FROM CONFLICT.

UNCOMMON WISDOM

Above all, clothe yourselves with love, which binds us all together in perfect harmony. And let the peace that comes from Christ rule in your hearts. For as members of one body you are called to live in peace. And always be thankful. —COLOSSIANS 3:14-15

UNCOMMON PRACTICE

Take a few moments to select one of this week's practices to explore further. The related Adventure Application appears just below each practice. If you'd prefer to come up with a different way of living out that practice this week, feel free to discuss what that might look like.

- *Watch what you say—even the truth can wound when it's spoken in the wrong way or at the wrong time.*
  What words have you said to your spouse this week that you wish you could take back? Why not run them by your husband or wife, asking for forgiveness if necessary?

- *Avoid frustration and seek to understand each other's heart by praying together and talking with each other.*
  On a scale of 1 to 10, how safe would each of you say you feel with the other? It's okay to admit that you've drifted far apart; in fact, when two people who care for each other confess their fears or lament the distance between them, they've taken the first step to a

closer relationship. If you don't feel safe—physically or emotionally—with your spouse, it's time to seek help from an outside counselor.

- *Practice thinking about an issue on which you disagree from your spouse's point of view.*
As you go about your daily tasks at home, do you find that you get irritated over the same type of issues with your spouse? If so, talk about what may drive your differences in those areas.

- *Don't assume your spouse understands how you feel— particularly when life gets busy.*
Whether you'd rate your marriage as strong or struggling, you and your spouse need to be on guard against anything that might get between you. Take a few minutes to discuss whether factors like busyness, hurt feelings, or misunderstandings are creating barriers between you. If so, begin talking through them. And don't be afraid to ask a wise Christian couple or counselor for help.

- *Be bold and speak the truth in love.*
Think about your communication pattern. Is it healthy? Are you able to be honest with each other without being destructive? Stay honest, but commit to remove sarcasm, disrespect, and other forms of "brutal honesty" from your conversations with your spouse.

- *Expect that when your emotions and perceptions don't line up, conflict will occur.*
Where are you looking? Down in defeat? At each other with eyes blazing? Or up to the one who promises that

you can do anything through Him? If you're not already looking up, how can you help each other do that?

UNCOMMON PRAYER

Take a few minutes to discuss any praises and needs you'd like to bring to God as a couple. Then, in addition to praying about those things together, use one or more of the following prayer prompts to seek God's help in resolving conflict constructively.

Praise God for His faithfulness, knowing that no conflict or problem is too big to navigate with His help.

Admit the specific struggles you face as you seek to build a marriage that isn't marked by conflict but by grace.

Ask the Holy Spirit to be your counselor this week, making Himself and His will known as you discuss difficult issues.

Thank the Lord that His love never ends and His patience never fails.

day 92
GETTING TO A WIN-WIN

CORE PRACTICE #79:
Resolve conflict by trying to understand each other and talking about the best way forward.

....

Don't be selfish; don't try to impress others. Be humble, thinking of others as better than yourselves. Don't look out only for your own interests, but take an interest in others, too. You must have the same attitude that Christ Jesus had.

Though he was God, he did not think of equality with God as something to cling to. Instead, he gave up his divine privileges; he took the humble position of a slave and was born as a human being.

—PHILIPPIANS 2:3-7

TONY

While in law school, our friend and cowriter Nathan took a course taught by Roger Fisher, a professor at Harvard Law School and director of the Harvard Negotiation Project. Fisher consulted on numerous negotiations aimed at brokering peace agreements in business and international politics around the nation and world. Fisher's book *Getting to Yes*, which introduced and outlined what Fisher called "principled negotiation" or "win-win negotiation," was the class textbook.

The essence of Fisher's approach was not necessarily to try to "win" the negotiation so that the other side was the loser, but instead to try and create the best possible win-win result that would benefit everyone.

To do that, he suggested you had to get past the individual positions and walls of difference that create conflict between parties, whether a husband and wife, two businesses, or two nations. He recommended exploring the interests and needs of both parties by considering questions like: Why does each want what they want? What are their fears in the situation? What do they hope to gain or accomplish in the end?

Although Lauren and I never attended this class, the wisdom of win-win negotiation is clear. We've always wanted to reach agreement when making decisions, but it took us a while to recognize how helpful it is to try to understand the why of our expressed "position." This leads to greater empathy between us and a willingness to try to come to a decision that satisfies us both. And that creates better harmony in our marriage overall.

In *Getting to Yes*, Fisher and coauthor William Ury illustrate how this might work by telling a brief story about two sisters who are fighting over an orange. Neither sister would budge— each wanted the whole orange. No one asked why. Finally, someone cut the orange in two and gave one half to each girl. The first sister peeled her half, threw away the rind, and ate the pulp. The other sister peeled her half, threw away the pulp, and ground the peel to use to make an orange cake. If someone had bothered to ask why they wanted the orange, each sister could have gotten the "whole orange"—either all of the fruit or all of the rind. That would have been an even better result.[26]

When Lauren and I take the time to explore what is important to us and why we feel the way we do about something, we're much more likely to reach a decision we can agree upon. We definitely get to know each other even better too. That's what we call a win-win!

Adventure Application: Beginning this week, practice exploring each other's viewpoint in any situation. Rather than digging in your heels, try putting yourself in your partner's shoes.

day 93
APOLOGY ACCEPTABLE

CORE PRACTICE #80:
Defuse tension during a minor disagreement by apologizing for your part.

....

And all of you, dress yourselves in humility as you relate to one another, for

"God opposes the proud
but favors the humble."

—1 PETER 5:5

Lauren

Two words can disarm any adversary and heal any bruised ego.

"I'm sorry."

When genuinely spoken, this simple phrase can be a powerful balm. That's especially true when you also follow Benjamin Franklin's advice to "never ruin an apology with an excuse." When offered outright and sincerely, without a qualifier like, "I'm sorry if what I said hurt you," these two words defuse any tension. When offered without a disclaimer like "What I meant to say was . . . ," they stand on their own and must be simply accepted or rejected for what they are—genuine remorse.

"I'm sorry." Nothing more is needed. Simply offer your apology in a conciliatory, loving tone.

I'm fortunate to be married to a man who is never afraid to say these two little words. Tony has an extraordinarily humble servant's heart for others, so he is able to see easily when "I'm sorry" is needed. When coming from Tony, those words are always real and always genuine. They never come with a justification for something he did or said. They aren't followed by an explanation that tries to explain away his behavior. If he has some rights he could point to, he doesn't try to stand on them. That has made him a wonderful example for me and our children through the years.

Tony seeks reconciliation because that is what Christ calls us to:

> All of this is a gift from God, who brought us back to himself through Christ. And God has given us this task of reconciling people to him. For God was in Christ, reconciling the world to himself, no longer counting people's sins against them. And he gave us this wonderful message of reconciliation. (2 Corinthians 5:18-19)

Christ came to earth, was crucified, and rose again so that we could be reconciled with Him and with each other, with the result being peace. When we choose to forgive and say we're sorry in marriage, we are modeling what the apostle Paul lays out in this passage. That's when healing takes place, love deepens, and peace reigns.

Of course, while saying "I'm sorry" may sound simple, it's not always easy to do. Yet in light of the impact it can have on our marriages and on those around us, it's definitely worthwhile.

We like Pastor John Piper's take on why forgiveness is so central to building a marriage. First, he points out that, because we are sinners, conflict is inevitable. Second, engaging in the "hard, rugged work" of forgiving actually makes renewing our affection for each other possible. Finally, God is glorified when "two very different and very imperfect people forge a life of faithfulness in the furnace of affliction by relying on Christ."[27]

So when we forgive each other, we're giving the world a taste of God's forgiveness for us. And that's nothing to be sorry about.

Adventure Application: Why don't you take a stab this week at being the person who makes peace reign in your home? When a disagreement or misunderstanding arises that leads you to act or speak too hastily, say "I'm sorry" as sincerely as possible. That's it. See what happens.

day 94
THINK POSITIVELY

CORE PRACTICE #81:
Maintain a positive attitude, even in tough times, by building friendships and finding activities you enjoy.

....

Fix your thoughts on what is true, and honorable, and right, and pure, and lovely, and admirable. Think about things that are excellent and worthy of praise. Keep putting into practice all you learned and received from me—everything you heard from me and saw me doing. Then the God of peace will be with you. —PHILIPPIANS 4:8-9

TONY

In his marvelous book *Expect to Win*, former Cleveland Browns defensive end Bill Glass recounts the story of the 1958 World Series between the Milwaukee Braves and the New York Yankees. Hall of Fame pitcher Warren Spahn was on the mound for the Braves in the sixth game, a game that could clinch the series for his team. The Braves were hanging on to a narrow lead when their manager called "time" and came out to the mound.

He told Spahn, "Whatever you do, don't throw it high and outside." Spahn, of course, knew that Elston Howard, the first African American player for the Yankees and a future Hall of Famer himself, was a great hitter of high, outside pitches. He shrugged—it was information he already had.

I'll leave it to you to figure where Spahn's next pitch was— high and outside, right in that sweet spot for Howard—who singled and eventually scored the winning run as the Yankees came back to win it all.

Spahn reportedly came off the field in a huff, remarking,

"Why would a manager tell you what he wanted you to do by telling you what not to do?"

The point is this—we tend to instinctively move in the direction of what our minds focus on and what we think will happen. How do you view your tomorrow? Is it positive or negative? What are your expectations for your tomorrow? Are they hopeful or full of despair?

May I suggest that you focus on what you want to occur—not on what you don't. You may not always get there, but you'll never reach your goal if you don't believe you can.

May I also suggest that, whenever possible, you do things with people who "carry a smile for their umbrella"—folks who have an optimistic outlook on life, folks who always see the glass as half full.

Lauren and I have decided that without an attitude of joy, expectancy, and possibility in every situation, we will miss the glorious moments God has planned for us. We encourage each other to set our minds on all He can and will do.

That isn't always easy. I remember a moment shortly before the end of the Buccaneers' 2001 season. Rumors were circulating that I might soon be replaced as head coach. I had just finished working out and was dressing in the coaches' locker room. A member of our front office staff was also there, getting ready for a run.

"Coach, I just wanted to say that I've appreciated seeing your witness in light of the circus that is occurring all around," he said.

With little time to consider my response, I said, "I think there are times when God welcomes the circus into our lives to give us an opportunity to show that there's another way to live and respond to things."

I don't think I could say it any better today.

What is your attitude right now? Whether you're experiencing good times or not-so-good times, remember that God is moving in your life and always wants the best for you. That means you have reason to be positive, right? Absolutely!

Adventure Application: This week, try to see everything with a can-do attitude. Agree that you'll commit yourselves to expect a positive outcome to life, even if your circumstances don't look positive right now. Then, several days from now, sit down again to talk about how that perspective affected your overall outlook.

day 95
MAKING THE MOST OF CONFLICT

CORE PRACTICE #82:
Don't fear conflict; use it as a tool to understand each other better.

....

Put on your new nature, and be renewed as you learn to know your Creator and become like him. In this new life . . . Christ is all that matters, and he lives in all of us. Since God chose you to be the holy people he loves, you must clothe yourselves with tenderhearted mercy, kindness, humility, gentleness, and patience. Make allowance for each other's faults, and forgive anyone who offends you. Remember, the Lord forgave you, so you must forgive others. —COLOSSIANS 3:10-13

Lauren
I find it ironic that some of the best experiences in life—getting married, having a baby, starting a new job, moving—often cause the most stress. Our family was excited about our move to Tampa in 1996, and about a year after Tony took the coaching job there, we began building a new home. The builder estimated it would take six to nine months to complete; in the end, it took almost nineteen months.

Stress, of course, can lead to conflict, and this was one time in our marriage when we found ourselves arguing more than usual. For the most part, our disagreements centered on minor issues like cost overruns and delays, but it was a good reminder that sometimes minor squabbles can create an undercurrent of tension in a marriage.

So does that mean couples should avoid conflict altogether? Conventional wisdom once said so, although over the past few decades some marriage experts dispute that. John Gottman, a psychologist who has spent forty years researching marriages, contends that couples who openly quarrel—sometimes loudly—may have strong marriages. The key seems to be validating the other person's emotions and being respectful even when the spouses strongly disagree with each other. Couples who regularly engage in personal criticism, contempt, defensiveness, or stonewalling, on the other hand, are likely to be unhappy.[28]

Of course, when most people hear the word *conflict*, they experience an uncomfortable visceral response. Yet as Gottman discovered, conflict can actually be a positive part of marriage. "We grow in our relationships by reconciling our differences," he says. "That's how we become more loving people and truly experience the fruits of marriage."[29]

During the five times we relocated during Tony's coaching career, we gained plenty of practice at defusing conflict. Moving wasn't all that easy on the children or me; fortunately, Tony was sensitive to the challenges the kids and I faced.

The two of us learned how important it was to "stay in the room" with each other so we could talk, listen, and really hear what the other was saying. Sometimes we even stopped to bathe our time of discussion in prayer. That usually defused the tension, and we were able to reconcile our differences relatively quickly. And each of us owned and supported the decision because we had given input and been heard.

No matter how long you've been married or how much you love and respect each other, conflict is inevitable. We've discovered it's never settled once and for all. And in that way it's somewhat like our house. Tony and I were so relieved when we finally moved our family into our new home in the summer of 1998 that we figured we had put any changes behind us. But as our family expanded, our house has had to as well.

Adventure Application: What's an area in which you've recently had conflict? If you have been afraid to reengage about any area in which you disagree, set aside enough time to allow each of you to express your heart on the matter. If you have trouble really listening to your spouse, keep a notepad nearby to make notes while listening. That way you will remember a point you want to come back to without interrupting your partner while he or she is speaking.

day 96
TOO FATIGUED TO FIGHT

CORE PRACTICE #83:
Don't try resolving major disagreements when you're tired.

Put on your new nature, created to be like God—truly righteous and holy. . . . And "don't sin by letting anger control you." Don't let the sun go down while you are still angry, for anger gives a foothold to the devil. . . . Don't use foul or abusive language. Let everything you say be good and helpful, so that your words will be an encouragement to those who hear them. —EPHESIANS 4:24, 26-27, 29

TONY

Nathan tells a story about a heated exchange late one night between him and his wife, Amy, early in their marriage. Amy, exhausted after a long day of teaching elementary school students, finally headed to the bedroom. Nathan followed her and began pacing around their bed.

Nathan doesn't recall the substance of the conflict or its ultimate resolution, but he remembers clearly standing over the bed and telling Amy, "The Bible says we aren't going to go to bed angry, so you should sit up and let's talk and figure this out!"

Two guesses as to what *didn't* get resolved that night.

And to make matters even worse, by the time Nathan gave up, he'd made matters worse with words spoken out of frustration, irritation, and fatigue. Lauren and I have learned all too well that at times, it's simply better to wait to resolve an issue.

On the other hand, we've long believed in not letting things fester. As the apostle Paul says in Ephesians, we shouldn't allow anything to drive a wedge between us. But we're not sure his admonition is designed to be ironclad. Yes, we need to take care of things in short order. We should not let an area of conflict grow and expand, taking on a life of its own. At the same time, God calls us to be wise. The end of a long day, when our weariness may be affecting our emotions, is often not the best time to try and interject reason into a conversation. We may just have to let go of our anger without resolving the situation. Paul doesn't say we have to solve every problem before the sun goes down, but that we shouldn't be angry with each other.

Some nights, Lauren and I have agreed to take a deep breath and wait until the next morning to talk through a disagreement. Things usually seem clearer when the sun is up and we're well rested. It may also be smart to wait to resolve conflict if you or your spouse is feeling under the weather or has experienced a great deal of stress on the job that day.

Lauren and I have come to realize that we love each other enough to avoid saying anything that we might regret when we're tired. In fact, while we give both Nathan and Amy credit for being willing to admit an area of disagreement, we think Amy may actually have been the wiser one that night long ago!

Adventure Application: Take a few minutes to discuss some times when it might not be best to try resolving a disagreement—whether late at night or in the car or just after either one of you gets home from work. Be sure to discuss the opposite too—when might be the best times to engage about areas of conflict?

day 97
GRACE IN GRIEF

CORE PRACTICE #84:
Allow each other to grieve differently, but be open to your spouse's need to talk.

....

All praise to God, the Father of our Lord Jesus Christ. God is our merciful Father and the source of all comfort. He comforts us in all our troubles so that we can comfort others. When they are troubled, we will be able to give them the same comfort God has given us. For the more we suffer for Christ, the more God will shower us with his comfort through Christ. —2 CORINTHIANS 1:3-5

Lauren

It's so hard to know what to say or to do when someone is grieving over the loss of a loved one. We are often concerned about intruding or maybe saying something that doesn't help or, even worse, is insensitive and upsets them.

For some reason, it doesn't seem any easier when the grieving person is a loved one. Even then, there are simply no magic words to take the pain of the loss away, which often leaves us feeling helpless. That is true even with two spouses who know and dearly love each other. But when we don't know what to say or do, Tony and I have learned the importance of making sure we're present for each other, even if we don't say a word.

The death of his mom and dad were deep personal losses for Tony. His parents molded and fashioned who he is, and I love how they helped nurture and grow him into the man he is today. He needed time to grieve their loss. It was the same for me when my dad passed away. Tony was so supportive, through listening to me and talking when I wanted, but he also gave me space when I needed it.

But the grief we experienced when we lost our son Jamie is beyond anything we could ever have imagined. Although we didn't understand why he took his life, we realized that God saw the whole picture, and we trusted Him to help us through this time of despair. Tony and I had spoken publicly about our Christian faith, praising God for all the good things in our life. Now that we were grieving, we realized we had an opportunity to stand up and say that, even though everything was far from great or perfect, we still trusted and loved the Lord. We knew that just as He had been with us in all the good and sad times in the past, He would be there for us in that most difficult time.

Our grieving was not by the clock. Tony and I had different moments of deep sorrow. At times, one of us seemed to do better on a particular day, only to be overcome by feelings of sadness the next day. We quickly learned to respect and support each other even when our feelings were far apart.

On those tough days, we could relate to C. S. Lewis's experience after the death of his wife, Joy:

> In grief nothing "stays put." One keeps on emerging from a phase, but it always recurs. Round and round. Everything repeats. Am I going in circles, or dare I hope I am on a spiral?
>
> But if a spiral, am I going up or down it?
>
> How often—will it be for always?—how often will the vast emptiness astonish me like a complete novelty and make me say, "I never realized my loss till this moment"?[30]

And, of course, in the moments of greatest despair, we clung most tightly to God's promises of comfort, such as the example in 2 Corinthians above. In the end, we realized that this was the only answer we had when we wondered how we would make it through a particular day—and, in the end, we realized it was enough to carry us through.

Adventure Application: Consider the quote from C. S. Lewis on page 235. How does it speak to you when it comes to the pain of dealing with your own grief or of reaching out to a friend, coworker, or acquaintance who has experienced a great loss?

day 98

PRINCIPLE 7

DON'T RUN AWAY FROM CONFLICT.

UNCOMMON WISDOM

Haughtiness goes before destruction;
  humility precedes honor.
Spouting off before listening to the facts
  is both shameful and foolish.
The human spirit can endure a sick body,
  but who can bear a crushed spirit?
Intelligent people are always ready to learn.
  Their ears are open for knowledge.

—PROVERBS 18:12-15

UNCOMMON PRACTICE

Take a few moments to select one of this week's practices to explore further. The related Adventure Application appears just below each practice. If you'd prefer to come up with a different way of living out that practice this week, feel free to discuss what that might look like.

- *Resolve conflict by trying to understand each other and talking about the best way forward.*
  Beginning this week, practice exploring each other's viewpoint in any situation. Rather than digging in your heels, try putting yourself in your partner's shoes.

- *Defuse tension during a minor disagreement by apologizing for your part.*

Why don't you take a stab this week at being the one who makes peace reign in your home? When a disagreement or misunderstanding arises that leads you to act or speak too hastily, say "I'm sorry" as sincerely as possible. That's it. See what happens.

- *Maintain a positive attitude, even in tough times, by building friendships and finding activities you enjoy.*
  This week, try to see everything with a can-do attitude. Agree that you'll commit yourselves to expect a positive outcome to life, even if your circumstances don't look positive right now. Then, several days from now, sit down again to talk about how that perspective affected your overall outlook.

- *Don't fear conflict; use it as a tool to understand each other better.*
  What's an area in which you've recently had conflict? If you have been afraid to reenage about any area in which you disagree, set aside enough time to allow each of you to express your heart on the matter. If you have trouble really listening to your spouse, keep a notepad nearby to make notes while listening. That way you will remember a point you want to come back to without interrupting your partner while he or she is speaking.

- *Don't try resolving major disagreements when you're tired.*
  Take a few minutes to discuss some times when it might not be best to try resolving a disagreement—whether late at night or in the car, or just after either one of you gets home from work. Be sure to discuss the opposite

too—when might be the best times to engage about areas of conflict?

- *Allow each other to grieve differently, but be open to your spouse's need to talk.*
Consider the quote from C. S. Lewis on page 235. How does it speak to you when it comes to the pain of dealing with your own grief or of reaching out to a friend, coworker, or acquaintance who has experienced a great loss?

UNCOMMON PRAYER

Take a few minutes to discuss any praises and needs you'd like to bring to God as a couple. Then, in addition to praying about those things together, use one or more of the following prayer prompts to seek God's help in resolving conflict constructively.

Praise God for going to such great lengths to restore your relationship with Him through the death and resurrection of His Son.

Admit your need for God's help and wisdom so that you can work through any present areas of disagreement or conflict between the two of you.

Ask the Holy Spirit to enable you to become a better listener so that you are better tuned in to His promptings, as well as to what your spouse's words and body language really mean.

Invite the Lord to shower you or other loved ones with His comfort following recent losses.

day 99
A LASTING LEGACY

CORE PRACTICE #85:
Consider what gifts, position, and influence God has given you as a platform to help other people.

....

But thank God! He has made us his captives and continues to lead us along in Christ's triumphal procession. Now he uses us to spread the knowledge of Christ everywhere, like a sweet perfume. —2 CORINTHIANS 2:14

TONY

In 2013, Hollywood released a movie that reminded the world of the incredible impact made by a man who had died over forty years before.

That film, *42*, centers on the first two years of Jackie Robinson's career with the Brooklyn Dodgers. In 1947 Robinson became the first African American to play major league baseball.

The movie picks up in 1945, shortly before the Dodgers' president, Branch Rickey, contacted Jackie about joining his team. Rickey was direct with Jackie about the possible consequences: "There's virtually nobody on our side. No owner, no umpires, very few newspapermen. And I'm afraid that many fans may be hostile. . . . We can win only if we can convince the world that I am doing this because you're a great ballplayer, and a fine gentleman."[31]

In fact, playing second base for a major league team was nothing compared to the insults, threats, and prejudice Jackie endured because he had dared to break baseball's color barrier.

Until the movie's release, many people were unaware of

the critical role Jackie's wife, Rachel, played during that time. Just one week after their wedding, she headed with Jackie to Daytona Beach, Florida, for his first year of spring training. As they traveled there by bus, these two California natives were shocked by the segregation they encountered. The difficulties only increased once they'd arrived in Florida. Still, Jackie played well during spring training and was assigned to the Montreal Royals, a Triple-A minor league team affiliated with the Dodgers. Six days before the start of the 1947 season, the Dodgers called Jackie up to play in the major leagues.

Rachel was well aware of the dangers her husband faced as he began his professional baseball career. She says she "always felt very protective toward him. I went to every home game." So how were they able to display such dignity and grace in public? Rachel recalls that they drove home together after games. During the drive, they spent time debriefing about any ugliness they'd seen and heard. "Before we got home, we had all those kinds of talks because home was a place where we needed to relax and not have to deal with the tensions of the outside world."[32]

Robinson played a total of ten seasons in the major leagues, finishing with a .311 batting average and a total of 1,518 hits and 137 home runs. His dignified character and undisputed talent changed professional sports for the better, but the pressures of breaking down baseball's color barrier took its toll. Jackie was just fifty-three when he died, and Rachel has been a steadfast advocate for her husband's memory ever since. As founder of the Jackie Robinson Foundation, she has overseen the distribution of thousands of college scholarships.

Nowadays, we hear a lot about a person's "platform." Rarely is it as visible or as dangerous as the one Jackie and Rachel Robinson assumed in the 1940s. And rarely has anyone used it more effectively either.

Whether we're in the public eye or not, however, we all have a platform. Using our occupations, our friendships, our families, and our accomplishments, we all are expected to impact and influence the world for the good of those around us and for God's glory. And as Jackie and Rachel illustrated so beautifully, God created marriage as a means for a husband and wife to support and encourage each other while fulfilling their unique purposes.

While you may not be making history like Jackie Robinson, never forget that God has given you an assignment with eternal consequences. According to the apostle Paul, you are to make sure you use your own gifts and platform "to spread the knowledge of Christ everywhere, like a sweet perfume." That's quite a lofty platform!

Adventure Application: We are each created by God with a unique purpose, passions, potential, and platform. This week, think about what those are for each of you. Talk about how you might use them to impact those around you for their good and His glory.

day 100

ABUNDANT GIVING, ABUNDANT LIVING

CORE PRACTICE #86:
Discover joy by giving to others in a way that suits you both.

....

But a poor widow came and put in two very small copper coins, worth only a few cents. Calling his disciples to him, Jesus said, "Truly I tell you, this poor widow has put more into the treasury than all the others. They all gave out of their wealth; but she, out of her poverty, put in everything—all she had to live on." —MARK 12:42-44, NIV

Lauren

Sharing with others has always been important to Tony and me. In fact, we started the Dungy Family Foundation with our extended families as a way to strengthen communities by providing opportunities for those in need.

By now, you probably know that one of the foundation's flagship programs is our reading program in Title I schools (those where at least 85 percent of the students qualify for free or reduced lunches) throughout Hillsborough County.

The reading program was actually the impetus for the first books Tony and I authored together. When we began visiting schools, we had difficulty finding books that were motivational and values based. It was also hard to find books with characters who looked like the children we visited and with story lines they could relate to. Since 2011, we've written over half a dozen children's books, each featuring our kids in fictional but true-to-life situations. When we occasionally bring Jade and Jordan with us on our school visits, the children are so excited to meet the real people the characters in our books are based on.

As much as the students and teachers seem to enjoy our visits, the joy we get from them is even greater. Yet it would be so easy to miss out on opportunities like this. The demands of parenting and running a household sometimes make me blind to the hurting people around me.

Giving of ourselves, it turns out, doesn't come naturally. Jesus made that clear as He commended the poor widow who gave everything she had as an offering to God. Under the religious regulations of the day, she would have been expected to give only one of the coins—worth a fraction of a penny—but she gave both. She was left with nothing.

Perhaps the disciples were more impressed by those who gave larger gifts. But Jesus wanted them to realize why, in His eyes, the widow's tiny gift was much more impressive. The others gave, but not to the point of extreme sacrifice. Most contributed more as an act of false piety than out of obedience to the rules of giving established by the local ruling body.

The Gospels don't tell us what happened to the poor widow, but we can be sure that God met her needs in some way that let her know He had seen and been pleased by her sacrifice. Even today, Christ calls us to sacrifice—not only our money, but our lives as well. How can you and your spouse partner in a way that costs you something? I can guarantee God will repay you with an overflowing amount of joy and fulfillment.

Adventure Application: When it comes to helping others, where do you and your spouse's passions intersect? Begin brainstorming a few ways you might reach out to someone in your community. If you already serve together, discuss how satisfied each of you are with that outreach.

day 101

LET THE LITTLE CHILDREN COME

CORE PRACTICE #87:
Use your resources and gifts in a way that glorifies God.

....

"Come, all of you who are gifted craftsmen. Construct everything that the LORD has commanded. . . ."All whose hearts were stirred and whose spirits were moved came and brought their sacred offerings to the LORD. They brought all the materials needed for the Tabernacle, for the performance of its rituals, and for the sacred garments. . . . So the people of Israel—every man and woman who was eager to help in the work the LORD had given them through Moses—brought their gifts and gave them freely to the LORD. —EXODUS 35:10, 21, 29

Lauren

My love for children started when I was a child myself. My sister and I ran a day care from our house when we were in junior high—an after-school program, really. We played games and provided craft projects for the children to complete, trying to create a fun environment.

Fun for them, fun for us.

When I met Tony, I had just finished my second year of teaching sixth grade. I'd initially hoped to teach younger children after I graduated, but when I was offered my first full-time job teaching older kids, it turned out that I loved working with them too.

I continued teaching after we were married, and then we added foster children to our home. More children! Now I was blessed with a number of children coming through our home, and I still had a classroom full of kids during the week.

Eventually, however, we decided to start our own family, and I decided to stop teaching in a classroom. In those early years of parenthood, I loved teaching and spending time with Tiara, Jamie, and Eric. It was a different season of life and a different way to use my gifts and our resources.

At times Tony and I have taught Sunday school or helped in our children's classrooms. Tony loves children as well, but his passions are not necessarily the same as mine. I don't think he'd necessarily seek out chances to teach grade-schoolers during church without me! But he has supported me in my interest, and I've been sensitive to him as well. (We didn't teach *every* week. . . .)

Then, when we were in Tampa with the Bucs, I felt called to adopt a child. The Lord had blessed us with the resources and given me the time, energy, and passion to do so. Tony agreed to at least look into it, since it was important to me, and now we've adopted six children. (Tony calls them our "second wave" of children!)

The passion God laid on my heart when He created me—a love for children—has manifested itself differently in the various seasons of my life. As a single woman it took one form; as a young wife, another; and I have continued to seek the Lord's guidance in how to be faithful to that passion as our lives change.

That initial gift has led to others. Tony is a terrific public speaker, but I've never particularly enjoyed it. However, over the years, I've had increasing opportunities to speak to groups about my passion for the adoption process. I've learned to embrace these engagements and have gotten comfortable with speaking to others, even if I still wouldn't call it a "gift" of mine!

Some of our gifts are obvious, and others we might embrace

a little more reluctantly—like Tony having a houseful of little kids or me speaking to a large audience. But through it all, the Lord calls on us to develop those gifts—and support our spouses as they use theirs.

Adventure Application: Take time to talk about which abilities and interests spark the most passion in each one of you. How well are you supporting one another as you seek to use those gifts?

day 102
REACHING OUT

CORE PRACTICE #88: Be hospitable.

....

*Don't forget to show hospitality to strangers, for some who have done
this have entertained angels without realizing it!* —HEBREWS 13:2

TONY

Lauren and I discovered that one of our favorite things about
being involved with the NFL was that it gave us plenty of
opportunities to be warm and welcoming to people in need.

When I became a head coach, requests for our help poured
in. Thankfully, my assistants—Lora McCarthy when I was with
the Bucs and Jackie Cooke when I was with the Colts—were a
huge help. They sorted through all the requests we received to
reach out to the ill or the needy, or to participate in a church or
nonprofit event. They knew the causes that were close to our
hearts—children, education and Christian outreach—and they
also knew which ones had a chance to fit into our schedules.

Of course, in reality, hospitality is often neither easy nor
convenient. Some interactions may even make us a little
uncomfortable. When the late Abe Brown first approached me
about visiting prison inmates with his ministry, I was pretty
nervous. But after my first few visits, I realized that these men
were as eager to hear about God's love as anyone on the outside.
Probably more so.

We can't always neatly pencil hospitality into our schedules
either. I learned this from Keli McGregor, whom I first met
when speaking at an Impact for Living conference several years
ago. Keli, former president of the Colorado Rockies baseball

team, passed away unexpectedly at the age of forty-seven. After his death, the stories that were shared of his hospitality were legion.

For instance, one day Keli and Dick Monfort, the owner of the Rockies, were headed to a meeting with a local Denver sports reporter to discuss the state of the franchise. On the drive there, they came upon a woman in a broken-down car. Even though Keli and Dick had a ready excuse—the meeting they needed to get to—the two men stopped to be sure her car was taken care of before they continued on to their meeting.

Keli had a similar experience on another day when he was running late to a meeting. As he drove down a Denver highway, he passed a muscular, tattoo-covered man changing a tire. Because the person looked capable of changing a tire on his own (not to mention that the man looked a little sketchy), Keli drove on. A few minutes later, however, Keli's conscience got the better of him. He pulled off at the next exit, swung around, and stopped at the car on the side of the road. Then he assisted the man with the tire.

Too often, men in particular assume that hospitality is only about serving tea and cookies. Yet any time we put ourselves out there to ensure someone else is comfortable, we are giving others a glimpse of God's grace. And as if that weren't enough, God says we may even be unknowingly interacting with angels!

Adventure Application: How can you and your spouse reach out and make a difference to someone this week?

day 103
LEARNING BY EXAMPLE

CORE PRACTICE #89: Model what a healthy marital relationship looks like to other young couples.

....

Don't let anyone think less of you because you are young. Be an example to all believers in what you say, in the way you live, in your love, your faith, and your purity. —1 TIMOTHY 4:12

Lauren

Teammates Donnie Shell and John Stallworth had a great impact on Tony when he was a rookie with the Steelers. Specifically, they helped him understand that God, not football, needed to be first in his life.

It's no surprise, then, that once we were married, Tony and I looked to Donnie and his wife, Paulette, and John and his wife, Flo, as role models for marriage. Ironically, by that point Tony was one of their coaches even though they were slightly older than him. Yet they were always gracious, and we all became fast friends. Looking back, they weren't *that* much older than we were. However, despite their relative youth, they were willing to step up and model what a strong marriage looks like.

In Kansas City, another couple, Leo and Yvette Morton, were instrumental in showing us how we could build up other young families by being welcoming. They were active in the community, but they also opened their home to their neighbors, which became a place where we all went to play games, watch movies, and eat meals.

All three couples taught us that no matter what your age or how long you've been married, you can live with a winsome, warm attitude that encourages other couples to look to you for help in building a strong marriage. That's why, over time, Tony and I also made it a point to invite other young families to our home to socialize.

In fact, when we arrived in Tampa, one of our goals was to intentionally and specifically model a healthy marriage for coaches, their wives, and especially players, both married and single. We let our players and coaches know we were there if they needed to talk. We thought it a privilege to be able to pray with them or to simply sit and talk with them.

That's why, when the Glazers invited me to attend road trips on the team plane, I jumped at the opportunity. While on the road, Tony and I held hands, talked, went for walks, and generally did our best to openly model a healthy, functioning marriage and family for the players. At the Glazers' invitation, we also began bringing our children on road trips during our second year with the team.

Even now that Tony has retired from coaching and taken up broadcasting, we look for opportunities to model a healthy marriage. In fact, that was really the point of writing *Uncommon Marriage*. We felt readers might not only enjoy learning our story, but they might learn something from both the good choices and the mistakes we've made over the years.

Though Tony and I wouldn't have felt qualified to write a marriage manual early on, inexperience has never prevented us from trying to teach by example. If we had waited until we had it all figured out, we'd never have gotten started. As Paul told Timothy in today's verse, just because you're young doesn't mean you don't have something worthwhile to share.

Adventure Application: Even though you probably don't feel that you have marriage all figured out, try to identify an area where you and your spouse might be a role model for another couple.

day 104
WHAT MATTERS MOST?

CORE PRACTICE #90: Don't spread yourself too thin; it's hard to serve well and joyfully when you're overcommitted.

When Moses' father-in-law saw all that Moses was doing for the people, he asked, "What are you really accomplishing here? Why are you trying to do all this alone while everyone stands around you from morning till evening?"

Moses replied, "Because the people come to me to get a ruling from God. When a dispute arises, they come to me, and I am the one who settles the case between the quarreling parties. I inform the people of God's decrees and give them his instructions."

"This is not good!" Moses' father-in-law exclaimed. "You're going to wear yourself out—and the people, too. This job is too heavy a burden for you to handle all by yourself." —EXODUS 18:14-18

TONY

I was fortunate to begin my career in the NFL with the Pittsburgh Steelers. During my ten years with that franchise—first as a player and then on the coaching staff—Coach Chuck Noll taught me the value of efficiency. He was all about getting work done in the right way, with the right attitude, and on time.

He also believed that his players and coaches should be well-rounded. That meant making family time a priority and finding other pursuits to learn from and enjoy. For him, that included flying planes, boating, and cooking.[33]

Over the years, I came to value Coach Noll's life lesson even more. It's easy to get so busy working that we either aren't as effective as we could be or we wear ourselves out. Perhaps the greater danger comes when we miss out on the important things of life. As the late Stephen Covey once wrote, we have to be able to distinguish between the "important" and the "urgent" tasks in life. Too many of us spend the bulk of our time dealing with the urgent—phone calls, paperwork, meetings—and forget that most good things in life fall in the important category.

Time devoted to our family, long-term goals, and prayer and Bible study all fall under the category of those activities that are important but not necessarily urgent. Without forethought, the immediate things that crop up will keep us from focusing on what matters most.

Moses was fortunate to have someone like Jethro point out how his priorities had gotten out of whack. Jethro helped his son-in-law determine which things only he could do and which he could delegate. In the end, Moses agreed to appoint some trustworthy men to take leadership over groups of Israelites and settle some everyday disputes.

As is clear from their conversation, the problem wasn't that Moses had taken on unimportant or bad tasks; rather, he had taken on too big a load, which was wearing him down and keeping his focus off what should have been his main concerns. Likewise, many of the activities that distract us aren't bad; it's just that they can crowd out higher priorities. It can happen all too easily: a worthwhile project, a great volunteer opportunity, "just one more thing that we need your help with" can distract us. In the process, we may start living by someone else's agenda and forsake our own. Take a lesson from Moses and Jethro, and don't let that happen to you.

Adventure Application: What is an area of importance that has been on the back burner too long and needs some attention from you? Are there steps you can take to make sure it gets the attention it deserves?

day 105

PRINCIPLE 8

SUPPORT EACH OTHER IN SERVING OTHERS.

....

UNCOMMON WISDOM

Give my greetings to Priscilla and Aquila, my co-workers in the ministry of Christ Jesus. In fact, they once risked their lives for me. I am thankful to them, and so are all the Gentile churches.

—ROMANS 16:3-4

UNCOMMON PRACTICE

Take a few moments to select one of this week's practices to explore further. The related Adventure Application appears just below each practice. If you'd prefer to come up with a different way of living out that practice this week, feel free to discuss what that might look like.

- *Consider what gifts, position, and influence God has given you as a platform to help other people.*
  We are each created by God with a unique purpose, passions, potential, and platform. This week, think about your own purpose, passion, potential, and platform. Talk about how you might use them to impact those around you for their good and His glory.

- *Discover joy by giving to others in a way that suits you both.*
  When it comes to helping others, where do you and your spouse's passions intersect? Set aside fifteen minutes

this week to talk with your spouse about the gifts and resources God has given you. Begin brainstorming a few ways you might reach out to someone in your community. If you already serve together, discuss how satisfied each of you are with that outreach.

- *Use your resources and gifts in a way that glorifies God.*
  Take time to talk about which abilities and interests spark the most passion in each one of you. How well are you supporting one another as you seek to use those gifts?

- *Be hospitable.*
  How can you and your spouse reach out and make a difference to someone this week?

- *Model what a healthy marital relationship looks like to other young couples.*
  Even though you probably don't feel that you have marriage all figured out, try to identify an area where you and your spouse might be a role model for another couple.

- *Don't spread yourself too thin; it's hard to serve well and joyfully when you're overcommitted.*
  What is an area that has been on the back burner too long and needs some attention from you? Are there steps you can take to make sure it gets the attention it deserves?

UNCOMMON PRAYER
Take a few minutes to discuss any praises and needs you'd like to bring to God as a couple. Then, in addition to praying about

those things, use one or more of the following prayer prompts to ask the Lord to enable you to serve together in ways that deepen your relationship and bring glory to Him.

Praise God for giving you individual gifts and personalities that you can use together to reach out to others.

Acknowledge your tendency—which all people share—to be so focused on your own problems, obligations, and schedule that you sometimes miss opportunities to help others.

Ask the Holy Spirit to point out the people He's put in your life to serve—and then ask Him for the grace and strength you need to obey His direction.

Seek the Lord's guidance in helping you see who needs hospitality— whether a simple greeting, a meal, or an act of service—this week.

Lift up the names of couples who may need to see what a healthy marital relationship looks like—perhaps because they are newly married or are struggling. Then ask God to show you how you and your spouse might be able to encourage them in their relationship in the coming days.

day 106
FOLLOWING THROUGH

CORE PRACTICE #91:
Remember that people are watching to see whether your actions and attitudes match your words.

You see, his faith and his actions worked together. His actions made his faith complete. —JAMES 2:22

Lauren

Have you ever struggled to "walk the walk" instead of simply "talking the talk"?

Tony had to face the consequences of falling short very publicly in 1999, his fourth season with the Bucs. Despite playing extremely well in a matchup against the New York Giants, the Bucs lost 17–13, due in part to a bad call by a referee near the end of the game. Tony criticized the officiating following the game, and he was fined for his remarks. Worse yet, he realized that his post-game criticisms didn't live up to his objective of building a culture of accountability and class. Tony was concerned that his remarks had undermined the very values he'd been advocating since coming to Tampa.

We all have reacted poorly to a situation, whether in front of our spouse, children, or friends. Often it's a sign that we need to better safeguard our hearts and minds by staying close to the Lord through regular Bible reading and prayer. In our own strength, it's impossible to "imitate Christ" (1 Corinthians 11:1); but these two spiritual disciplines keep our hearts aligned with His.

If you struggle with walking your talk, a good Scripture to

study is James 2. There, James, the brother of Jesus, reminds believers that true faith is accompanied by Christlike actions. In chapter 2, verses 21 through 26, James points to two biblical examples whose words and actions were in harmony. The first is Abraham, who lived out his faith by his willingness to sacrifice Isaac if God commanded it. The second figure held up as a model may surprise you. Rahab, a prostitute from the ancient city of Jericho, is praised for hiding the Hebrew messengers who had come to scout her city just before the Israelites entered the Promised Land.

Rahab told the spies that all of Jericho's inhabitants had heard about how God had delivered the Israelites from the pursuing Egyptians at the Red Sea, as well as how the Israelites had defeated two Amorite kings. Then she proclaimed, "The LORD your God is the supreme God of the heavens above and the earth below" (Joshua 2:11).

James isn't commending her for her words alone. Amazingly, even before she made her public declaration, she had refused to turn over the Israelite messengers when the king demanded that she do so.

The writer of Hebrews explains how her faith and action worked together: "It was by faith that Rahab the prostitute was not destroyed with the people in her city who refused to obey God. For she had given a friendly welcome to the spies" (11:31).

While we should strive to be like Abraham and Rahab, we will fall short sometimes. After all, each one of us has been guilty sometime of talking the talk but not walking the talk.

Adventure Application: Is there an area with which you have struggled to make your actions meet your words? Pray with your spouse about it.

day 107
AN EXAM WORTH TAKING

CORE PRACTICE #92:
Be open to signals from your spouse that you are overcommitted.

....

Therefore, I urge you, brothers and sisters, in view of God's mercy, to
offer your bodies as a living sacrifice, holy and pleasing to God—this is
your true and proper worship. Do not conform to the pattern of this
world, but be transformed by the renewing of your mind. Then you will
be able to test and approve what God's will is—his good, pleasing and
perfect will. —ROMANS 12:1-2, NIV

TONY

Taking stock of where you are physically, emotionally, and spiritually is time well spent.

After all, mechanics give your car regular tune-ups, your dentist checks your teeth once or twice a year, and doctors administer annual physical exams. Some of the check-ups are mental: Children have parent-teacher conferences at regular intervals, and who hasn't sat through a performance review at work?

But when is the last time you stopped as a husband and a wife to assess whether you are really living up to your values and priorities?

I am blessed to have Lauren help me regularly assess whether my actions are aligned with my priorities. When I was coaching, for instance, I often struggled to find enough time to spend with our children. I'd do well for a while, but then she'd tell me that one of our children was asking, "Why has Daddy been gone so much?"

As helpful as those reminders were, they came *after* I had already missed out on time spent with them. But how could I give my children the time they needed if I was overcommitted at work, or in volunteer or community service activities? The short and honest answer?

I couldn't.

And so I am suggesting that you and I take seriously the admonition to examine our lives and then see if they are consistent with what God wants us to do.

I heard a dear friend share at a gathering not too long ago that one day you and I are going to come face-to-face with the reality that we can't do our life over again—one time around is all we get! Though I knew that to be true, his words hit me right between the eyes. I have just one shot at leaving a legacy for my wife and children by being a part of their lives. The alternative is leaving a trail of regrets stemming from missed moments and opportunities, as well as misdirected priorities. What matters more? To leave a legacy of material success—trophies, homes, cars, and awards—or to leave a legacy of fingerprints on the hearts of those I love most?

I encourage you to sit down with your spouse to examine your lives. Ask yourselves whether your marriage is as close as you'd like it to be. What is your purpose as a couple, and how well are you living it out? Are you pouring into your children's lives in the way they need? What will your legacy be? What will people say about you (or about me) when we are gone? What do we want them to say at our memorial services?

We shouldn't begin considering these questions in our last days. It is something we should think about and live out every day.

Is it time to examine your life?

Adventure Application: Take a few moments to each list your priorities. Then compare your lists to determine how closely they align—and spend time in frank discussion about how well you are living up to the goals that matter most to you.

day 108
STAY OUT OF THE PIT

CORE PRACTICE #93:
Keep your priorities straight: put faith and family first.

....

The LORD grants wisdom! From his mouth come knowledge and understanding. —PROVERBS 2:6

Lauren

The view from the top of the Grand Canyon is breathtaking. In places, the gorge is eighteen miles across and, in others, a mile deep. It's quite a reminder of the majesty of God's creation.

But that chasm didn't develop overnight. It was cut into the rock by water from the Colorado River, beginning its journey in the Rocky Mountains and eventually making its way into the Gulf of California and then the Pacific Ocean.

Water wearing down rock. Little by little. Most of it invisible to the naked eye as it happens. Just wearing it down.

That happens with our lives too. We know what matters to us. And then, so often, other things start to encroach on our time and our attention. Tony saw coaches spend a little extra time in the office one day to catch up or get ahead. Not a bad thing.

And then they did it again. And again. And then that "little more time" became the new normal. And then they tried to get ahead again by staying even later.

It's not just men. I've watched women do it too. We start down a particular path, make an exception, and then the exception becomes the rule.

People have the amazing ability to acclimate, and the ability to adapt is critical as we grow and change. I remember when Tony and I were first married. We were both working at the time and found it relatively easy to live within our means. A few years later, I stopped teaching to stay home full time with Tiara. We were down to one income. That required an initial adjustment, but we acclimated to it.

We acclimated to other changes, too. When Tony worked with the Kansas City Chiefs, the coaching staff was expected to work much longer hours than he'd been used to doing in Pittsburgh. As a result, he had less time to spend with our children. After an initial adjustment, however, that became our new normal.

The danger, of course, is that these adjustments—sometimes imperceptible at first—widen until the day you find yourself staring into a chasm eighteen miles wide and a mile deep.

The good news: We can redirect our actions again. When we do, we may be startled by the positive change in our lives. I remember how, during the first few weeks after Tony's retirement, the kids would come home and ask, "Is Dad still here?" They were so excited that he wouldn't be going anywhere. And Tony happily slipped into the role of being a full-time dad—at least for a time.

You don't have to wait for retirement or to make a job change to reset your course. I encourage you to refresh yourself and your family by taking a look at your priorities at regular intervals.

Don't wait until you're staring into a pit that looks too deep to pull yourselves out of.

Adventure Application: Establish some preappointed times to meet to discuss how well you're living by the priorities you've set for your family. You might choose to do this monthly, making a note on the calendar for each designated time. Schedule your first check-in within the next two weeks.

day 109
TIME AND TALENT MANAGEMENT

CORE PRACTICE #94: Consider what only you can do when deciding where to volunteer or what causes to support.

....

Therefore, whenever we have the opportunity, we should do good to everyone—especially to those in the family of faith. —GALATIANS 6:10

TONY

Tom Lamphere, chaplain of the Minnesota Vikings, is a close friend of mine and has played a special role as a counselor for me ever since I coached in Minnesota in the early 1990s. Among many words of wisdom he has provided, he made the point that while there are plenty of things I could do to help people, many of those could be done just as well by someone else.

That's true for all of us.

God has given us all different gifts and put us in different positions to help other people and organizations. The key to maximizing our impact is to focus on helping in those areas that mesh with our particular gifts.

For example, I have always enjoyed public speaking, and coaching helped me develop that skill, so speaking engagements have seemed like a good use of my gifts. I can use a hammer, but it's not my strong suit. So taking a day to build homes with Habitat for Humanity might be noble, but it probably wouldn't be too productive. In fact, it might take more people to undo the damage I would cause. At the same time, however, I can't possibly accept every speaking engagement I'm offered.

At each stop in my career, Lauren and I tried to discern how

I could maximize my impact while still maintaining sufficient time for my responsibilities as an employee, father, and husband.

It wasn't easy because there were so many great charitable organizations that we could support. Every organization that has reached out to me is striving to make a positive impact and has participants who passionately believe in the mission.

After I retired from coaching, I had even more difficulty with this. I was excited to have more free time to volunteer, but after a year, Lauren sat me down. "Tony, we are in danger of seeing less of you than we did when you were coaching. All of these causes are wonderful, but you're going to wear yourself out and shortchange your family as well." And she was right. Her counsel was wise.

Just because I had more free time did not mean the two of us could be any less judicious in deciding which activities and organizations to assist. As Tom had told me eighteen years earlier, I still needed to figure out which things only I could do and which ones someone else could easily do as well as or better.

God wants us to give of our time, and I am not trying to discourage people from doing that. We've all seen how hard it can be to get volunteers for church or other charitable events. Ultimately, however, our primary focus should be on our faith and our family, and we have to understand that we're not indispensable. If someone else is as well-equipped as we are to take on a task, we should think long and hard about letting that other person do it.

After all, the Lord of the universe is in control of it all!

Adventure Application: You and your spouse *should* be engaged in the world around you. But take a few minutes to take stock of both of your activities. Are you overcommitted? Are there things that you could let someone else do?

day 110
HIS AND HERS

CORE PRACTICE #95:
Focus on both partners' passions.

....

Just as our bodies have many parts and each part has a special function,
so it is with Christ's body. We are many parts of one body, and we all
belong to each other. —ROMANS 12:4-5

Lauren

When we met, Tony was immersed in sports. I wasn't nearly as passionate about them, but I decided to buy in and go along with that lifestyle because it meant I could spend more time with Tony.

In the same way, Tony has always tried to connect with me and my interests. Tony loves children but probably not in the same way that I *love* children. But he stays open and sensitive to that passion of mine.

All of us have been given passions by the Lord, those things that excite us, that get us out of bed, that energize us after a long day of fielding phone calls, working through a desk covered in paperwork, or shuttling children all over town.

But just because the "dating" phase has ended and the marriage has begun, it is no less important to continue exploring each other's interests and passions. In fact, it's probably *more* important to continue to look for those after the marriage. Too many couples end up buying that second television and escaping to different rooms after dinner, spending the evening in the solitude of their own interests.

It's easy to pursue our own passions, but one of the keys to keeping a relationship healthy is to stay focused on the passions of the other person. She might like action movies while you prefer romantic comedies. He might like eating out after church on Sundays, while she might look forward to spending the afternoon eating at home. Or one of you might prefer hiking or exploring nearby parks, while the other is, as Nathan Whitaker calls himself, an avid indoorsman.

We've seen some couples model how to accommodate each other's passions. One couple we know compromised by traveling to the home games of the husband's college alma mater in the fall and then taking regular weekend visits to the beach—her interest—every spring and summer. Rather than being resentful when traveling to the other's preferred destination, each has embraced his or her interests.

We know of another couple who moved to the Spanish coast because the wife said she wanted to experience raising their children for a year in another culture. Since his wife had followed him around during the twenty years he'd spent in corporate America, her husband agreed. They sold their Tampa home and headed overseas. After nine months, even she had experienced enough, and they raced back to the United States and have settled in Austin, Texas.

The important thing is to remain open, listen to each other, and maybe every now and then watch an action movie, whether you want to . . . or not.

Adventure Application: What are some ways, big and small, that you can help your spouse explore a passion?

day 111

IN THE SPOTLIGHT

CORE PRACTICE #96: Share the spotlight with your spouse whenever you receive credit or recognition.

....

Let someone else praise you, not your own mouth—
a stranger, not your own lips.

—PROVERBS 27:2

TONY

I've enjoyed positions that at times have caused people to single me out for attention. Sometimes Lauren spotted the potential traps more quickly than I did. People she didn't know would come speak to her at church, eventually getting around to asking, "So what's new with the Colts?" She'd usually just shrug.

We both got used to people expressing so much interest in my position that if I wasn't careful, I'd start feeling "special." In essence, we have to walk a fine line. God did create us all to be unique—that is reinforced in Scripture. But He didn't make any of us more special. If we ever begin feeling that we are, that's a bad path to start down. It's really dangerous when it involves a marriage.

I look at this principle more broadly, too. Sometimes the best thing we can do when opportunities come our way is to share the experiences. So many times the Lord has opened doors that I could have walked through alone, I suppose, but I enjoy them more when I walk through them with Lauren.

When I became the head coach of the Tampa Bay Buccaneers, I was suddenly in demand to serve on committees and boards and to speak on behalf of the team around town. I enjoyed representing the team in this way, but I knew how important it was for Lauren to be involved also.

At first, she wasn't sure I was doing her any favors, especially when it came to public speaking! As Lauren has mentioned, she preferred working behind the scenes and led the way in community service. But over time, she got more comfortable with public speaking and did more of it. And that was important because I always wanted people to see what a big part she played in the success of our team, especially off the field.

The most visible time we were able to share the spotlight came immediately after the Colts won the Super Bowl in February 2007. Lauren sat through the pouring rain in the stands, watching us come back from a rough start (and a questionable coaching decision by me) to win the game. The week before, she and I had discussed what I would say in a post-game interview, and before I knew it, Jim Irsay, the team's owner, had escorted her to the field and she was on the podium next to me.

Sure enough, I was asked—with her standing beside me—about how it felt to be the first African American coach to lead a team to a Super Bowl victory. I said that while I was honored to have that distinction, I was especially proud that we'd done it the Lord's way, by embracing family and the values that last and are truly meaningful.

Lauren was with me, sharing the moment. It was perfect.

To me, sharing the spotlight is a mind-set. The opportunities and achievements aren't all about me; they're about us. If I'm looking for ways to recognize the importance of the two of us operating as a unit, I have to look for ways to include Lauren in any "spotlight" that might come along.

Adventure Application: What upcoming opportunity might you share with your spouse? Something that would be more effective—maybe double the impact or fun—if you were both involved?

day 112

PRINCIPLE 8

SUPPORT EACH OTHER IN SERVING OTHERS.

....

UNCOMMON WISDOM

Seek the Kingdom of God above all else, and live righteously, and he will give you everything you need. —MATTHEW 6:33

UNCOMMON PRACTICE

Take a few moments to select one of this week's practices to explore further. The related Adventure Application appears just below each practice. If you'd prefer to come up with a different way of living out that practice this week, feel free to discuss what that might look like.

- *Remember that people are watching to see whether your actions and attitudes match your words.*
  Is there an area with which you have struggled to make your actions meet your words? Pray with your spouse about it.

- *Be open to signals from your spouse that you are overcommitted.*
  Take a few moments to each list your priorities. Then compare your lists to determine how closely they align—and spend time in frank discussion about how well you are living up to the goals that matter most to you.

- *Keep your priorities straight: put faith and family first.*
  Establish some preappointed times to meet to discuss how well you're living by the priorities you've set for your family. You might choose to do this monthly, making a note on the calendar for each designated time. Schedule your first check-in within the next two weeks.

- *Consider what only you can do when deciding where to volunteer or what causes to support.*
  You and your spouse *should* be engaged in the world around you. But take a few minutes to take stock of both of your activities. Are you overcommitted? Are there things that you could let someone else do?

- *Focus on both partners' passions.*
  What are some ways, big and small, that you can help your spouse explore a passion?

- *Share the spotlight with your spouse whenever you receive credit or recognition.*
  What upcoming opportunity might you share with your spouse? Something that would be more effective—maybe double the impact or fun—if you were both involved?

UNCOMMON PRAYER

Take a few minutes to discuss any praises and needs you'd like to bring to God as a couple. Then, in addition to praying about those things, use one or more of the following prayer prompts to ask the Lord to enable you to serve together in ways that deepen your relationship and bring glory to Him.

Praise God for creating you with a need for rest and reflection—which are opportunities to look to Him for strength and renewal.

Confess the ways you've tried to live up to standards set by our culture or your own desire to get ahead to the detriment of your own or your family's well-being.

Ask the Holy Spirit to help you set priorities that will maximize the strengths and abilities He's given you as well as the impact you can make on your family, your church, and your community.

Seek the Lord's help as you try to determine "what only you can do" when seeking opportunities to serve outside your family.

Thank the Lord for your spouse and for the specific ways in which he or she has helped you accomplish your objectives, nurtured you and your children, and kept your household running smoothly.

Ask the Lord to remind you of any principles in this book that will ensure your marriage continues to be both uncommon and a life-giving adventure!

ENDNOTES

1. Gary Chapman, "In-Laws: God's Blessing," *The 5 Love Languages* (blog), November 24, 2008 http://www.5lovelanguages.com/2008/11/in-laws-gods-blessing/ (accessed May 21, 2014).
2. Viktor Frankl, *Man's Search for Meaning* (Boston: Beacon Press, 2006), 66.
3. *Merriam-Webster's Collegiate Dictionary*, 11th ed., s.v. "identity."
4. Galatians 5:22-23
5. Bruce Feiler, "Can Gary Chapman Save Your Marriage?" *New York Times*, November 19, 2011.
6. Ibid.
7. Based on an anecdote at "Marriage," Sermon Illustrations, originally published in *Bits & Pieces*, August 22, 1991, http://www.sermonillustrations.com/a-z/m/marriage.htm.
8. Ecclesiastes 3:1
9. Jimmy Van Heusen and Sammy Cahn, "All the Way," Maraville Music, 1957.
10. Don Meredith, "What Does God Say about Marriage and Sex?" in Joe Gibbs, *Game Plan for Life* (Carol Stream, IL: Tyndale, 2009), 170–171.
11. Drew Brees, *Coming Back Stronger* (Carol Stream, IL: Tyndale, 2010), 103–104.
12. Angela Hicks, "10 Little Things Connected Couples Do," *Prevention*, November 2011, http://www.prevention.com/sex/sex-relationships/10-little-things-connected-couples-do/3-ask-question-every-day.
13. Erin Strout, "Better with Age," *Running Times*, January/February 2013, http://www.runnersworld.com/elite-runners/better-age?page=single.
14. Ibid.
15. Gary Chapman, *The 5 Love Languages* (Chicago: Moody, 1992).
16. "No Good Thing," Stories/Jokes at smalleymarriage.com. See http://www.smalleymarriage.com/resources/stories.php?catID=35&resID=304#res_top. Scripture quoted in story is Psalm 84:11, KJV.
17. Susan Donaldson James, "Deciding to Marry a Quadriplegic: Couple Tells Love Story," ABC News, May 30, 2013, http://abcnews.go.com/Health/deciding-marry-quadriplegic-couple-tells-love-story/story?id=19282468.
18. Paul F. Boller Jr., *Presidential Wives: An Anecdotal History* (New York: Oxford University Press, 1988), 119.
19. John George Nicolay, *An Oral History of Abraham Lincoln: John G. Nicolay's Interviews and Essays*, ed. Michael Burlingam (Carbondale, IL: Southern Illinois University, 1996), 128.

20. Erwin W. Lutzer, *Making the Best of a Bad Decision* (Carol Stream, IL: Tyndale, 2011), 58.

21. See 1 Samuel 24:44 and 2 Samuel 3:15.

22. Shaunti Feldhahn, *The Surprising Secrets of Highly Happy Marriages* (Colorado Springs: Multnomah, 2013).

23. Tony Evans, "Handling Marital Conflict with the Power of Christ," *The Kingdom Agenda* (blog), June 4, 2012, http://go.tonyevans.org/blog/bid /162109/Handling-Marital-Conflict-with-the-Power-of-Christ

24. Ibid.

25. "On Stereotypes, Risks, and Jesus: Driscoll Interviews Piper," *Resurgence* (blog), http://theresurgence.com/2012/12/11/on-stereotypes-risks -and-jesus-driscoll-interviews-piper/.

26. Roger Fisher and William Ury, in chapter 4 of *Getting to Yes: Negotiating Agreement without Giving In* (New York: Penguin Books, 2011).

27. John Piper, "Marriage: Forbearing and Forgiving," sermon, February 18, 2007, http://www.desiringgod.org/sermons/marriage-forgiving-and-forbearing.

28. John Gottman and Nan Silver, "What Makes Marriage Work?" *Psychology Today*, March 1, 1994, http://www.psychologytoday.com/articles/200910 /what-makes-marriage-work.

29. Ibid.

30. C. S. Lewis, *A Grief Observed* (New York: HarperOne, 1996), 56–57.

31. "Quotes about Jackie Robinson," Jackie Robinson: The Official Website, http://www.jackierobinson.com/about/quotes.html.

32. Cynthia Lee, "Rachel Robinson to Receive UCLA's Highest Honor," UCLA Newsroom, May 5, 2009, http://newsroom.ucla.edu/stories/rachel-robinson -to-receive-ucla-90830. See also Kostya Kennedy, "Rachel Robinson Reflects on Her Life with Jackie and the Movie *42*," *Sports Illustrated*, April 11, 2013.

33. See more at: http://www.success.com/article/tony-dungys-championship -life#sthash.42MEKhsh.dpuf

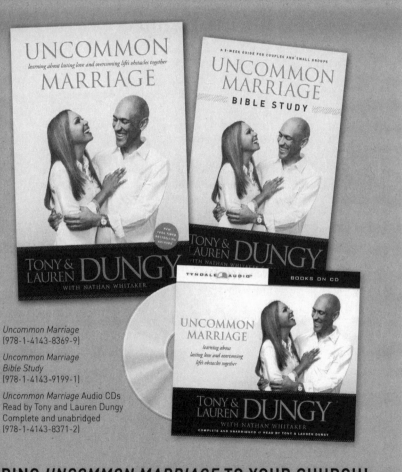

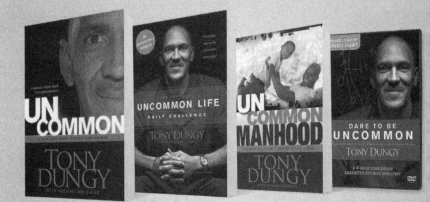

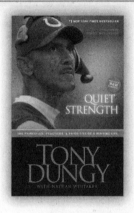
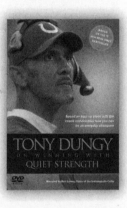
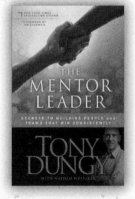

Tony and Lauren Dungy bring together their faith, love of children, and love of sports to tell stories of inspiration and encouragement.